A PARENTS' GUIDE
TO THE
NEW CURRICULUM

Michael Baker is the Education Correspondent for BBC TV News and Current Affairs, and is an expert in the changing field of educational policy and practice. He has also written for the *Guardian* and the *Listener*. He lives in Kingston-upon-Thames, Surrey.

A PARENTS' GUIDE TO THE NEW CURRICULUM

Michael Baker

BBC BOOKS

For Louise and Rachel

Published by BBC Books,
a division of BBC Enterprises Limited,
Woodlands, 80 Wood Lane, London W12 0TT

First published 1992
© Michael Baker 1992
The moral right of the author has been asserted

ISBN 0 563 36306 1

Set in 10/11pt Ehrhardt by
Phoenix Typesetting, Chatham, Kent

Printed and bound in Great Britain by
Clays Ltd, St Ives plc

Cover printed by Clays Ltd, St Ives plc

CONTENTS

■

ACKNOWLEDGEMENTS

It is impossible to mention individually all those who have helped me in the writing of this book, but I am grateful to them all. However I would like to thank Paul McGill and all the subject specialists at the National Curriculum Council for their advice. The staff at the Schools Examination and Assessment Council and the Department of Education Press Office have also patiently answered my enquiries. Special thanks must go to the heads and teachers in all those schools which have allowed me through their doors – usually followed by a television crew. Any errors are, of course, my own. I would also like to thank Heather Holden-Brown, Julia Wigg and Richard Gay at BBC Books and my colleagues in BBC TV News.

My parents – who have both spent very full careers in education – deserve special thanks for giving me an interest in the subject. I must also thank my daughters – Louise and Rachel – for giving me the benefit of a parent's view of schools and my wife, Chrissy, for . . . well, everything.

I
SCHOOLS
TODAY
■

WHAT TYPES OF SCHOOLS ARE THERE?
WHO IS IN CHARGE?
THE EDUCATION REFORM ACT

Few things are more all-consuming for parents than working out how to do the best for their children's education. Which school to choose? How to be sure children are doing as well as they should? How to help them to do better? These and many other questions can hang like a dark cloud over conscientious parents. They were never easy to answer. But they are particularly hard for parents to grapple with when schools – and the curriculum in them – are changing so fast. Our schools are only just emerging from the biggest shake-up for over 40 years. Its often been traumatic for schools and teachers and puzzling, to say the least, for parents. The organisation of schools, the subjects taught and the methods used now are often very different from when today's parents were sitting behind their own school desks.

At the best of times, understanding the education system can feel like painting the Forth Bridge. The task is never complete. No sooner have you absorbed how schools are run and who makes which decisions than it has all changed again. At least, that is how it can appear. But after the biggest upheaval for decades, the dust is now beginning to settle and a clearer picture is emerging. This is particularly true of the new National Curriculum. Whatever political changes happen in the next few years, it seems that the new curriculum – if nothing else – is here to stay.

This book is designed to help parents find their way through the educational maze. Later sections will deal specifically with what children will be taught and how they will be tested. But before getting inside a school, it helps to know what types of schools are available, who runs them, and what sort of education they offer.

■ TYPES OF SCHOOL
There are around 35,000 schools in the United Kingdom, catering for some nine million children. Of these the vast majority are nursery and primary schools (26,000) or secondary schools (5,000) in the state sector. These are known as 'maintained schools'. In other words, they provide free education and are funded – or maintained – out of national and local taxation. Over 90 per cent of children attend maintained schools. The remainder attend independent schools.

TYPES OF STATE SCHOOL
County Schools set up and run by the local education authority.
Voluntary Schools originally provided by voluntary bodies (mainly churches) which still meet some costs, but now mainly funded by the local education authority.
Grant Maintained Schools – these have opted out of local authority control and are funded directly by central government.
Special Schools owned and run by the local education authorities to cater for children with special educational needs.

Primary Schools
Children normally begin school when they are five, although many schools take children at the start of the term or year in which they reach that age. Almost all primary schools take both boys and girls. The most common division is into *infant* schools for children aged five to seven and *junior* schools for seven to 11 year-olds. However in some parts of the country education authorities have a system of *first* and *middle* schools. These are for children from five to eight/nine and from eight/nine to 12/13. Because this age pattern does not sit comfortably with the new curriculum, several authorities are considering returning to the standard pattern of pupils changing from primary to secondary school at 11.

Secondary Schools
Children must attend secondary school until the age of 16. The usual starting age is 11, but in areas still operating a *first, middle* and *upper*

school system, pupils move on to the final stage at 12 or 13. After that, about 20 per cent of 16 to 18-year-olds remain in schools and a further 35 per cent continue their education outside schools on both full-time and part-time college courses. For those who do remain at school, it is usual to stay for a further two years until the age of 18, although some pupils carry on for just one extra year. Pupils over 16 can choose to continue their education at *Sixth Form Colleges*, which are effectively schools consisting only of sixth forms, or at *Further Education* or *Tertiary Colleges*, which provide a range of full-time and part-time courses, as well as traditional A Level studies.

Most parts of the country still have a choice of girls-only, boys-only and co-educational schools. But that choice is disappearing fast as more and more schools have closed or been merged because of the falling number of secondary-age pupils. (The number of children at primary schools is, in contrast, rising, making it more difficult for parents to get the school of their choice.) As numbers fell, it was often convenient for councils to reduce surplus places by requiring local boys' and girls' schools to merge. Girls-only schools have been dwindling fast and in England there are now only around 250 left.

The most common type of school is the *comprehensive* which caters for youngsters of all abilities. *Grammar* schools select the most able pupils, usually on the basis of standardised tests in verbal reasoning and on the recommendations of primary school head teachers. In all but a few areas, pupils must be amongst the most intelligent 20 to 25 per cent of their age-group to get in. Where there are only a few grammar schools left, selection is even tougher than that. Only around 150 grammar schools remain. The main areas where the selective system still survives are: Kent (29), Lincolnshire (15), Buckinghamshire (14), Essex (8), Devon (8) and Dorset (7). Some outer London boroughs – such as Bexley, Kingston-upon-Thames, Redbridge, and Sutton – have also retained a few grammar schools.

Fee-charging Schools
There are around 2,500 schools in the United Kingdom which are independent of local and national government. They educate over 600,000 children. Their income comes mainly from fees charged to parents and from endowments. Some schools are run like businesses for private profit, but the larger, better-known schools are usually charitable foundations. All independent schools must be registered with the government and must meet basic legal requirements for

their standards of health, fire safety and buildings. The government used to inspect independent schools in order to certify them as 'efficient'. This no longer happens, although the national schools inspectorate (HMI) does still occasionally visit non-state schools. One form of accreditation is provided by the Independent Schools Joint Council which inspects schools in a similar fashion to HMI.

■ WHO IS IN CHARGE?
The decisions which affect your child in school are made at a number of levels. It helps to know who is responsible for which decisions, not least so that you know where to take any complaints. At the top in England is the Secretary of State for Education and his civil service department, the Department of Education and Science. The Welsh, Scottish and Northern Ireland Secretaries of State and their Departments fill the same roles outside England. At the next level are the Local Education Authorities, responsible for ensuring there is adequate schooling in their area. Then – at school level – there are the individual governing bodies, head teachers and classroom teachers.

WHO MAKES THE DECISIONS?
National level
The Department of Education and Science (England).
The Welsh Office.
The Scottish Office.
The Northern Ireland Office.

Local level
The Local Education Authorities:
England: County Councils, Metropolitan Districts,
   London Boroughs.
Wales: County Councils.
Scotland: Regional Councils.
N. Ireland: Education Boards

School level
Governing bodies including head teachers.

One *Education Secretary* complained recently that he employed no teachers and owned no schools. However the holder of this Cabinet post has considerable influence, not least the power to veto any proposals to reorganise or close schools. More significantly, the Education Secretary sets national educational policy. Either through advice or encouragement or by using legal powers, the Education Secretary can determine the way schools are run, pupils are taught and teachers trained. The Education Secetary also has the final say over the National Curriculum and testing.

Indeed – so long as the government has a clear majority in Parliament – there is relatively little that an Education Secretary cannot legally impose given sufficient time.

THE EDUCATION SECRETARY
- sets government policy on education.
- can veto proposals to reorganise or close schools.
- approve plans for the National Curriculum and testing.
- is responsible for the supply and training of teachers.
- is responsible for national educational standards.

Despite the power of central government, most schools are actually run by the *Local Education Authorities*. They are responsible for ensuring that the education system is working within their area. There are 116 of them in England and Wales. They are elected councils – counties, metropolitan districts and London boroughs – with other functions in addition to education. Although the full council has the final say, the key decisions are usually taken by an education committee. This is made up of elected councillors and others appointed to represent special interests such as the churches.

The education committee usually reflects the balance of power on the full council and is normally led by a councillor from the ruling Party. Your local Town Hall will give you the names of members of the committee and you can write to them there. Meetings are open to the public. A strong turn-out of parents on sensitive issues like school closures can influence decisions. Politicians want to be re-elected, so let them know if you disagree with decisions affecting education in your area.

Day-to-day running of schools within the local education authority is the responsibility of a *Chief Education Officer* or *Director of Education*, who is an employee of the local authority. Any enquiries about schools in your area should be addressed to the Education Office at the County or Borough headquarters. You can find the address and telephone numbers of your local education authority –

and a list of all its secondary schools – in your local telephone directory or in the Education Year Book. The latter is updated each year and should be available in your local library.

Although their powers have been much reduced recently, the education authorities retain an important role which affects children and parents. Their main responsibility is to ensure 'efficient education' and a school place for all children in their area. The quality of education provided – and the amount spent on each child – varies from one part of the country to another. There are some areas of education where councils can choose whether or not to spend money, for example in nursery education. So, not surprisingly, parents will find that the availability of nursery schooling varies enormously from one education authority to another.

LOCAL EDUCATION AUTHORITIES MUST PROVIDE
- for the educational needs of the local population.
- budgets for schools from locally-raised revenue and central government grant.
- transport to schools where necessary.
- help for children with special educational needs.
- information on schools.
- an opportunity for parents to state school preferences.

At school level the *Governing Body* is in overall charge, with the head teacher responsible for day-to-day management. The governors balance the budget, appoint staff and set policy on such issues as sex education and discipline. The governing body is made up of elected parent governors, appointed local authority representatives, teachers and head teachers and other members appointed for their special knowledge. The numbers of each vary according to the size of the school. The political representatives appointed by the local authority cannot be in the majority, and there must be a minimum of two parent-governors and one teacher-governor. You will have the opportunity to vote in elections for parent governors or even to stand for election. In *Scotland*, the equivalent of governing bodies are *School Boards*. These have a majority of parents and are responsible for managing their school.

The governing body must meet at least once in each term. It must also make an annual report to parents and hold an annual parents' meeting to discuss that report. You should try to attend since the governors' decisions will affect your child. The role and power of governors has been increased considerably in recent years.

RESPONSIBILITIES OF GOVERNING BODIES

- ensuring the National Curriculum and assessments are followed.
- ensuring the law on religious education and collective worship is followed.
- drawing up a policy on sex education.
- making provision for pupils with special needs.
- deciding how to spend the school's budget and keeping accounts.
- selection, discipline and dismissal of staff.

If you are unhappy with any of these matters at your school you should let the governors know, although it is best to discuss them with the head teacher first. The school secretary will give you their names and help you contact them.

■ THE 1988 EDUCATION REFORM ACT

It is hardly surprising that the education world was knocked into a spin by the Education Reform Act. It made a sudden and wide-ranging impact on schools. The aim was to change fundamentally the nature of education in England and Wales. It is, without doubt, the largest and most important piece of legislation affecting education since 1944. Below are some of the most important changes.

The National Curriculum

The Education Reform Act established the first ever National Curriculum in England and Wales. The aim was to ensure that all pupils followed a broad range of basic subjects whether they lived in Cornwall or Cumbria. It makes certain subjects compulsory for all pupils in state schools from the age of five to 16. It also lays down the content of the courses pupils must follow for each subject and sets the targets of knowledge against which they will be tested.

The National Curriculum is compulsory in all state schools. It is not required by law in independent schools, but in practice most of them will follow it. It is made up of three 'core' subjects and seven further 'foundation' subjects, plus Welsh in Wales.

The Education Reform Act also requires pupils to be tested on their performance in the National Curriculum at the ages of seven,

11, 14 and 16. More details of this – and of the curriculum itself – are given in the chapter on tests and exams and in those covering each subject.

NATIONAL CURRICULUM SUBJECTS
Core Subjects
- mathematics
- English
- science.
- Welsh (only in Welsh-speaking schools in Wales)

Foundation Subjects
- history
- geography
- technology
- music
- art
- physical education
- a modern foreign language (in secondary schools only).
- Welsh (only in schools in Wales which are not Welsh-speaking).

Religious Education

Although it is not part of the National Curriculum, religious education is also compulsory for all pupils, including sixth-formers. Each education authority syllabus will continue to be decided locally by Standing Advisory Committees on Religious Education which must include representatives of all the main religious groups in the area, Christian and non-Christian.

RELIGIOUS REQUIREMENTS
- all pupils in school must be given religious education.
- all schools must provide daily religious worship.
- religion must be mainly Christian in character.

The biggest change is that any new syllabus for religious education must be mainly Christian in character. This requirement has upset many members of non-Christian religions in Britain and some have cited it as one of the reasons why Muslims want their own state-funded schools.

The daily act of worship – or religious assembly – normally remains compulsory for all pupils and it too must be mainly

Christian, but parents can still ask to withdraw their child from both religious education and school worship. Whole schools too can request permission to opt out of the requirement for mainly Christian worship. To do so, they must consult governors and parents and get permission from their local advisory committee. This might apply where a large proportion of pupils at a school are from minority religions. Individual assemblies may also be non-Christian provided that over the whole school term the predominant pattern is of Christian worship. In other words, schools can still hold a Muslim or Sikh assembly on an occasional basis.

The Act does not require the whole school to be involved in an act of worship together. Many schools hold assemblies on a class, year or tutor-group basis. Schools are also free to hold their act of worship at any time during the school day, not just at the start. In general, more traditional schools tend to maintain the practice of whole-school assemblies at the start of the school day. Others take a more flexible approach.

Choice of Schools

The law now gives parents the right to state their choice of school and to have that choice met as long as the school in question is not full. Parents do not have to choose the nearest school or even one belonging to the education authority they live in. Nor do they have to give reasons for their choice.

This is known as *open enrolment*. It has done away with artificial catchment areas set by local education authorities so they – not parents – could decide which school children go to. According to ministers, the intention is to increase parental choice and to 'reinforce successful schools and give others an incentive to improve'.

OPEN ENROLMENT REQUIRES THAT
- wherever possible parents get the school of their choice.
- the only limit on pupil numbers is the physical capacity of buildings.
- education authorities cannot interfere with admission arrangements.

Who decides when a school is full?
Under the new rules, a school is full when it has reached what is known as the 'standard number' of pupils. For secondary schools this

is usually based on the number of pupils at the school in 1979 when numbers were at their peak. In primary schools it is usually based either on the number of pupils attending the school in 1990–1 or on a formula based on the physical space in the school, whichever is the greater. Schools may – if they wish – take more than the standard number but they cannot turn pupils away if they have not yet reached it. Nursery classes are not covered by the requirement, but reception classes are.

Voluntary-aided schools (such as Church of England or Roman Catholic schools) are given some freedom to ensure they can 'preserve the character' of the school. In other words, they are able to agree with the education authority the number of non-Catholics or non-Church of England pupils they will accept. Grammar schools are also given special treatment to allow them to keep their selective character.

Open enrolment is designed to ensure that schools are responsive to the preferences of parents, in much the same way as businesses must respond to consumer demand. In the past, local education authorities sometimes restricted places in popular schools in order to ensure an even spread of pupils throughout the schools in the area. This is no longer allowed. The old policy meant that some schools avoided closure and it prevented class sizes growing too large in popular schools. In practice, the vast majority of parents did get the school of their choice under the old system. Now that education authorities can no longer plan strategically, it is possible that popular schools will be full to the brim while less popular schools could close, thus reducing choice.

There is another problem. While parents will clearly welcome increased choice, there is bound to be frustration if that freedom of choice proves to be illusory. This will be the case when popular schools are oversubscribed. Then difficult decisions have to be taken on how to determine which pupils to accept and which to reject. It will usually be done on the basis of the distance between school and home, except where other factors come into play such as a child already attending a linked nursery school or having a brother or sister already at the school. This frustration is likely to be strong if parents find the only school with places left for their children is an unpopular one or one that is a long way from home.

If you are not offered the school of your choice, you have the right to appeal. Further details are given in the chapter on parents' rights (see pages 187–195).

School Budgets

Schools are now in charge of their own spending. Whereas in the past they had to get permission from their education authority to spend even quite small sums, they now have complete control over their budgets. For a large secondary school that could be two or three million pounds a year. Local Management of Schools – as this is known – has meant a big increase in the financial responsibilities of both head teachers and governors. It also makes it easier for parents to lobby for particular use of school funds. Initially smaller primary schools were exempt from LMS, but from April 1994 all schools must have control of their budgets.

LOCAL MANAGEMENT OF SCHOOLS REQUIRES
- schools to take control of their own budgets, like small businesses.
- education authorities to fund schools according to the number of pupils they have.
- school governors to 'hire and fire' staff.

Even more important than who controls the money is the way the school's income is determined. This is important since it will affect class sizes and the availability of new books and equipment. At its most extreme, it could even determine whether or not a school can survive. Funding is now based mainly on the number of pupils at the school. The idea is to tie funding to a school's popularity, so a growing school will get more money and a school that has falling numbers of pupils will get less. In effect, this means that every pupil through the front gate carries a price tag.

The logic behind this change is that schools will try harder to satisfy parents in order to attract the maximum possible number of pupils and so ensure the highest possible income. Schools which are unpopular with parents would – it is argued – either have to change their ways or live within a dwindling budget. However there is concern that this pupil-based formula will lead either to larger classes or a tendency to recruit younger and cheaper teachers in order to balance income and outgoings. Opponents of the scheme also point out that pupil numbers can rise and fall for simple reasons like a change in the birth-rate. They say the resulting fluctuation in income will make school budgeting difficult.

Opting out

The Education Reform Act gave schools the freedom to break away from the control of local education authorities. A sizeable minority has already done so. This is known as 'opting-out'. It requires the support of a majority of parents in a secret ballot. Once a school has left local authority control, it is funded by grants directly from central government. It is then known as a *Grant Maintained School*. Its grant is based on what it would have got from the local authority, but with one important difference. This is an extra 15 per cent to make up for the services previously provided by the local authority. These services – such as advisory teachers or the use of swimming pools or field study centres – must now be bought by opted-out schools.

Apart from this change, these schools remain state schools, funded by taxation and free for pupils. They must provide the National Curriculum like other state schools. They also retain their former character as either comprehensives or selective schools. They can apply to change their status, but this requires a further ballot of parents. Within this limitation, they have one other important freedom – they can set their own criteria for admitting pupils.

WHAT IS A GRANT MAINTAINED SCHOOL?
- it has left the control of the local education authority.
- it is run by the school's governors.
- it gets its money directly from central government.
- it remains a state school, providing free education.
- it gets more money, but must purchase previously free services.
- it has greater freedom over the way it selects its pupils.
- it must still follow the National Curriculum.

Since all schools are now taking over control of their own budgets, why should any wish to opt out? One possible advantage is the extra money schools get to cover centrally provided services. They can now choose to buy these or to spend the money on other things instead. On the other hand if a large number of schools opt out from one authority, it may no longer be able to provide many of its former services. Opted-out schools also have greater freedom to set their own criteria for accepting pupils. For some schools, opting out has been a way of avoiding closure, merger or loss of grammar school status. This has made it difficult for education authorities to remove costly 'surplus' school places.

What difference does opting out make?

As a parent, opting out could affect you in a number of ways. You may be unhappy with decisions taken by the education authority which would change the nature of your child's school. For example, the authority may decide to merge a girls-only school with a neighbouring boys-only school. If you – and other parents – are unhappy about that you may decide to ask the school governors to hold a ballot of parents in order to become a Grant Maintained School and preserve the current position. Or you may simply feel unhappy with the way your local authority is running its schools. Again you as a parent could decide to start the process by which the school will be freed from the influence of the local authority. On the other hand, you may feel that the local authority is doing a good job and is providing services (such as library loans, special needs, school meals, educational psychology) which the school cannot provide as efficiently on its own.

2
PRIMARY
SCHOOL
∎

■ **FINDING OUT ABOUT PRIMARY SCHOOLS**
When to start looking
Although you do not need to follow the daft practice of putting your child's name down for a school at birth – as applies in some fee-charging schools (usually with non-returnable deposits) – it is never too early to start finding out about primary schools in your area. It may be that none of them match your expectations or simply that they are all further from home than you would like. In which case, there may still be time to move house or even to take out a savings policy to pay for private education.

Nursery education
A more common reason for looking early is to find out about nursery education. Not all primary schools have nursery classes and not all areas are well provided with state nursery schools. Some councils provide nursery education for around 90 per cent of three and four year-olds. Others have places for only about ten per cent. So, for

example, the chance of your getting free nursery education for your child is far better on Tyneside than it is in West Sussex. This is because education authorities are not legally required to provide education for children under five. Despite all the evidence suggesting the educational value of an early start, nursery education remains at the whim of education authorities.

PROPORTION OF THREE AND FOUR YEAR-OLDS IN STATE EDUCATION IN 1990

Over 80 per cent	*Under 25 per cent*
South Tyneside	Surrey
Walsall	Hereford and Worcester
North Tyneside	Hampshire
Salford	Essex
Liverpool	Buckinghamshire
	Wiltshire
	Oxfordshire
	Kent
	Bromley
	West Sussex

Good nursery education is important in itself, but it also has implications for the next stage. A place in a nursery class or a nursery school attached to a primary school will often ensure a place at that school later on. Also the transition from nursery school/class to primary school will be easier for your child if they stay on the same site and if their friends move with them.

Where local authority nursery education is widely available, children may be admitted at the age of three or occasionally even younger. So you should put your child's name down for nursery education before he or she is two. You should do this by contacting the school itself. This means, unfortunately, that you should already be finding out about the primary schools your child will go on to.

Admission to primary school

For those parents who either cannot get or do not want nursery education, decisions can be delayed a little longer. By law, education must begin at five and education authorities must provide all children with a school place no later than the start of the term after their fifth birthday. The precise age at which schools take children varies from one area to another. It is common for children to go to school at the start of the term in which they will become five. This is known as taking 'rising fives'. A growing trend is to admit children just once a year. They then take children who will be five within that school year (September to August). So summer-born children will start school in the autumn not long after their fourth birthday.

You can find out about schools' admissions policy from the local education authority, whose address and number is in the telephone directory or at the local library. This information will explain the local procedures for the move from nursery classes or schools to the primary school. It will also explain whether your child will initially attend primary school full or part-time. Because of the difference between a child who is five in September and one whose fifth birthday is not until the following summer, many authorities start the younger children on mornings or afternoons only. They then switch to full-time schooling in the term in which they become five.

Getting Information

The first step is to find out the total range of options within your area. Your local education authority will provide a full list of its primary and nursery schools, including their admissions policies. If you live close to the border with a neighbouring authority you should request information on its schools too. This information will cover infant schools (ages five to seven), junior schools (seven to 11), 'all through' primary schools (five to 11), and nursery schools where they exist. Where authorities operate a system of first (five to eight/nine) and middle (eight/nine to 12/13) schools, information will be available on these. It should give the name, address and telephone number, head teacher's name, number of pupils on the roll, and the number to be admitted next year for each school.

For more detailed information contact schools directly and ask for a prospectus. This should give information on the schools' aims, facilities, its policies on discipline, uniform and the curriculum, and details of the school's governing body. You might also wish to obtain a copy of the annual report of the School Governors and you could enquire – of both the school and the local authority – whether there are any recent reports by local authority inspectors or Her Majesty's Inspectorate of Schools which affect the schools you are interested in. HMI reports are available free of charge from: Department of Education and Science, Publications Despatch Centre, Honeypot Lane, Stanmore, Middlesex HA7 1AZ.

INFORMATION PROVIDED IN A PRIMARY SCHOOL PROSPECTUS
- names of the governing body.
- a list of the school staff.
- the aims of the school.
- general information on numbers, ages of pupils and size of accommodation.
- whether there is an attached nursery school or class.
- policy on religious instruction, sex education, and special needs.
- after-school clubs and activities.
- the hours of the school day.
- policy on discipline and uniform.
- policy on parental involvement in the school.

How to apply

The next step is to contact the schools you are interested in and request an application form. This usually has to be returned to the school of your first choice, although it will also allow you to state other preferences. The precise deadline for applications will, again, be obtainable from your local authority. However you should expect to be completing your form in the January or February before the start of the school year (September) in which your child will become five, or two years earlier if you are applying to a primary school with a nursery class or a separate nursery school.

■ FEE-CHARGING SCHOOLS

What is available?

You may wish to consider what is available in the independent sector of education at primary level. Broadly speaking, these schools fall into two main categories: the pre-preparatory schools (for ages two to seven) and junior or preparatory schools (seven to 11 or 13). The 'preparatory' title is explained by the fact that the last two years are usually spent preparing children for the Common Entrance examination for entry to senior schools. However there is usually no reason why children should not leave at 11 to go to state secondary schools, except where a preparatory school is linked with or part of an independent secondary school.

The best starting point to find out about fee-charging schools is the annual guide produced by the Independent Schools Information

Service. ISIS is part of the Independent Schools Joint Council and covers around 1,400 fee-charging schools. The guide gives the name and address of schools, their entry requirements, age range, numbers of pupils and – particularly important – the level of fees. It also includes very clear advice on how to select the best independent school for your child. ISIS can be contacted at: 56 Buckingham Gate, London SW1E 6AG, or by telephone on 071–630–8793/4.

Fee-charging schools come in a variety of forms. Some are privately owned and run for profit. The biggest – and the best –are more usually charitable foundations. Around 7.5 per cent of the school population attends independent schools. As well as the mainstream preparatory schools, there are also religious schools, choir schools, schools for gifted children or those with special needs, and schools devoted to 'alternative' educational philosophies.

What will it cost?
School fees can prove very expensive, particularly if you have more than one child and if they remain at fee-charging schools until 18. For example, it has been estimated that for a child starting school in 1996 at five and staying until 18, parents will have to find average fees of around £140,000. Fees have been rising faster than inflation in recent years. In 1991, for example, they rose on average by 12.5 per cent. For pre-preparatory schools, fees for 1992 range from approximately £1,000 to £2,300 a year and for preparatory schools they range from £2,000 to £5,500 a year for day-pupils and from £4,500 to £8,000 for boarders. Senior schools cost even more. These are only the basic fees. Many schools will charge extra for lunches, individual musical instrument tuition, medical supplies, school trips etc. Parents should ask about these 'extras' when choosing a school. There are several specialist school fees financial advisers, many of which advertise in the ISIS guide.

School fees are beyond the means of most parents. However financial help may be available through scholarships and bursaries. These range from paying full fees to contributing just a few hundred pounds. There are specialist scholarships available for children with a particular musical or artistic talent. Details of choral scholarships are available from the Choir Schools' Association. One other point is that many of the best independent schools will be oversubscribed, so registering your interest early is advisable. Your child will also have to satisfy entrance requirements. These vary, but most schools rely on a combination of interview, informal assessment and written test.

Why Choose A Fee-Charging School?

This, of course, is a highly selective matter. Surveys have shown that common reasons for selecting an independent school include educational standards, discipline, dissatisfaction with state schools, and smaller classes. Many parents will of course choose independent schools simply because that has been the tradition in their family. However there is an increasing number of 'first-time buyers', where neither parent attended an independent school themselves. A common mistake, though, is to assume that just because a school charges fees it is necessarily better than a state school. This is not so. Independent schools probably include some of the best and some of the worst schools in the country. There are fewer checks on independent schools and staff do not even have to be qualified teachers. As with all decisions about schools, it is less a matter of selecting the 'best' school (if such a thing exists) than of finding the right school for your child.

■ HOW TO CHOOSE A PRIMARY SCHOOL

Choosing a school is one of the hardest things parents face after the birth of their children. I know because I recently went through the process with my eldest daughter. The first factor to consider was distance from home. This was not only a practical consideration, but also a realistic one. In my area – as in many parts of the country – there are rising numbers of children of primary school age. Many schools are oversubscribed and therefore select pupils mainly on the basis of distance between home and school. This factor effectively narrowed the choice to two infant schools. However I also had to take into account that these fed into adjoining junior schools. While it may be possible to transfer at the age of seven, that cannot be guaranteed and in any case my daughter would probably be unhappy if she were separated from her friends mid-way through primary school. So the choice was not simply between two infant schools, but also between two junior schools.

The next step was to visit all four schools we were interested in. Schools usually have a local reputation, but this is based on unreliable hearsay. A school may have gone through a rough patch because of the nature of a previous head teacher's leadership. That reputation will linger even after a new head teacher has arrived and changed things. So while it is always worth talking to parents of children currently at the school you are considering, anyone else's opinion

WHAT TO LOOK FOR IN A PRIMARY SCHOOL

- are the children busy and occupied?
- is there an atmosphere of purposeful learning? (This is not necessarily the same as children sitting silently at their desks.)
- do teachers seem in control and relating well to the children?
- is the teaching done in groups or to the whole class?
- is there lots of work on display?
- look at children's workbooks. Is there a variety of work and constructive comments from the teacher?
- what is the decorative state of the classroom?
- are the classrooms open-plan or separated?
- are there plenty of attractive books available for children?
- is there much scientific equipment?
- how many computers are there?
- is there evidence of art and design work and materials?
- how many children are there in each classroom?
- are there nursery nurses or assistant teachers in the classrooms?
- are there sports/cooking/music facilities and equipment?
- is there a quiet area for reading?
- does the school provide hot meals at lunchtime?
- what state is the playground in?
- is there a playing field?

QUESTIONS TO ASK AT A PRIMARY SCHOOL

- what are the school's aims?
- is there a nursery class?
- at what age will they take your child and do they begin by attending for half-days only?
- what are the class sizes?
- are there mixed-age classes, with a range of more than a year?
- are childen grouped by ability for activity work within classes?
- what approach is taken to teaching reading?
- what is the level of staff turn-over?
- are there staff shortages?
- is the school growing or declining in size?
- which secondary schools do most pupils go on to?
- does the head teacher expect to be staying for long?
- are parents encouraged to help in the classroom?
- is there an active Parents' Association?
- is special emphasis put on music/sport/the creative arts etc?

must be carefully weighed. In the end the best thing to do is visit the school for yourself.

Any good school will be happy to show you around. The way the school treats your request – and the trouble they take in answering your questions – is a good guide to the self-confidence of the school and its staff. Most schools will see parents either individually or in small groups and show them round the school. Make sure your visit is during the school day. You want to see teaching in action not empty desks. Head teachers will usually see prospective parents themselves. It is important to meet the head teacher since he or she will be the single most important influence on the nature of the school. It is always worth asking them how long they have been at the school and how long they intend to stay. There is little point in being very impressed by a head teacher if he or she is planning to leave next term.

At one school I visited the head teacher saw about six parents together. Between us we fired question after question at him. At one point he said he felt as if he were attending a job interview. To which one father quickly retorted that he was! The head teacher – to his credit – readily accepted that he was being assessed for his suitability for the post of educator-in-chief of our children. Many parents, though, are unsure what questions to ask and what to look for. They feel unqualified for the task. They should not: it is mostly a matter of getting a feel for a well-run school. Do not be rushed and do not be afraid to take a written list of the questions you want to ask. There is no definitive checklist of things to ask or look out for, but on the left – in no particular order – are some suggestions.

■ WHAT MAKES A GOOD SCHOOL?
While most parents will want to trust their own judgment, it is useful to know what the experts think makes a good school. One major study by five educationalists set out to find out what difference schooling made to children quite apart from other factors such as their home background. It followed a group of 2000 pupils through four years in the classroom from age seven to 11 between 1980 and 1984. *School Matters: The Junior Years* by Peter Mortimore and others (Open Books Publishing Ltd, 1988) found that 'all-through' schools where children did not have to transfer at the age of seven were at an advantage. It also found that voluntary-aided schools and schools with fewer than 160 pupils on the junior roll did better (although this may

no longer be true with the National Curriculum). It also found that class size made a difference. Smaller classes with fewer than 24 pupils had a positive impact on younger pupils, whereas in classes with 27 or more pupils the effects were not so good. Other positive factors included: a good physical environment; a stable teaching staff; continuity with one class teacher throughout the year; a head teacher who has been at the school for between three and seven years.

The authors of *School Matters* also identified twelve key factors lying within the control of the staff which are crucial to a school's effectiveness. These are:

★ purposeful leadership by the head teacher.

★ an established deputy head able to assume delegated responsibilities.

★ teachers given a say in the way the school is run.

★ consistency between teachers in their approach to teaching.

★ structured classroom work, with pupils given some autonomy but within a clear framework.

★ intellectually stimulating talk between teachers and pupils.

★ work-centred classrooms with a high level of pupil activity and low noise levels.

★ lessons that focus on one, or at most two, areas of the curriculum at a time.

★ emphasis on communication between teachers and the whole class as well as with individuals (but the authors say they do not advocate a return to traditional teaching).

★ good record keeping of pupil's progress.

★ parental involvement in schools and at home.

★ emphasis on praising and rewarding pupils, rather than punishing them.

The most important finding of the *School Matters* report was that the school really did make a difference. It argued that although a school cannot remove fundamental differences such as inherited intelligence and home background, the performance of children was significantly affected by the effectiveness of their school. So – it argued – disadvantaged children at a good school could end up with higher achievements than more advantaged children at less effective schools. The authors also believed that the years between seven and 11 were particularly important since children are still able to change their view of themselves as good or poor learners.

■ TRADITIONAL OR PROGRESSIVE?

No parent who regularly reads newspapers can fail to have been worried by some of the headlines and stories which have suggested that our schools are in the hands of cranks, trendies and progressives. Certain newspapers paint a picture of liberal, airy-fairy, free-for-all, doctrinaire schools which they contrast with the formal, ordered, disciplined approach of the past. Needless to say, this is an oversimplification. Tabloid journalism requires quick, simple labels. Reality is not quite like that. Nevertheless there have been big changes in the style of and approach to primary school teaching over the past few decades and some have caused concern. The debate has been fuelled by a major study of primary teaching in Leeds by Professor Robin Alexander of Leeds University. This has raised doubts about the effectiveness of some of the teaching methods which have become normal practice. It shows how the widespread commitment to group work, to thematic approaches and enquiry modes of teaching 'may present some teachers with problems of classroom organization which subvert the quality of children's learning and frustrate teachers' monitoring of that learning' (*Primary Education in Leeds* by Robin Alexander, University of Leeds 1991).

Education ministers have seized on the Alexander report and are using it to argue against so-called 'progressive' teaching methods. One minister talked of the 'obsession with topics and projects' saying this turned many schools into playgrounds with 'much happiness and painting, but very little learning'. Professor Alexander himself, though, has warned against polarising the debate into 'formal/ traditional' and 'informal/progressive' terms, which he says would be simplistic and unhelpful.

Nevertheless, the tide may be turning. The General Secretary of the National Association of Headteachers, David Hart, said recently that the time may now have come for a change to subject-based teaching, by specialist teachers, for nine to 11 year-olds. This would be a big change since most primary classes are taken by one teacher all the time, with several subjects often approached through a single topic or theme. Mr Hart also suggested that junior schools should reconsider streaming or setting pupils by ability, an approach currently out of fashion in primary schools.

Why are children often taught in groups?

When today's parents were at school, classrooms were probably characterised by straight rows of desks filling the entire available space. Now it is much more common for desks or tables to be arranged in groups of four or six. There are also likely to be areas of the classroom set aside for specific activities. A 'quiet area' for reading is common. There might also be a 'science area'. For very young children there is often a carpeted area where the whole class gathers at the start of the day or while the teacher explains the tasks they will be undertaking. This sort of classroom layout has developed because it is better suited to teaching children in groups.

Group work is much more common today than 20 or 30 years ago. Teachers organise pupils into groups for many reasons, including:

★ it is often the best way of using limited equipment, such as computers.

★ they can offer a wider range of activities, tailored to children's abilities and needs.

★ it can be a better way for children to develop and practise skills.

★ it allows the teacher to give one-to-one tuition while others are busy working on tasks.

Child-centred or subject-centred?
This less formal approach has been characterised as 'child-centred learning'. It is a label which makes many teachers feel uneasy, since they would argue that all teaching is aimed at the child and takes into account the individual abilities of each. They argue that child-centred teaching does not amount to letting children do as they like. But it has been strongly attacked by some critics. One has called it the 'Blue Peter' approach to the curriculum, characterised by progress-ive ideas sustained by 'romanticism' and too much emphasis on arts, crafts and creativity and not enough on factual knowledge or spelling and grammar.

So what is child-centred education? It is based on a belief that pupils learn best by discovering answers for themselves. This does not mean they are left to educate themselves, but there is greater emphasis on involvement in activities and on finding answers for themselves. Some say it is hard to make this approach work in large classes. They prefer what has been called a 'subject-centred' approach, where the teaching is based on getting children to learn factual content. This approach is characterised by whole-class teaching. But leading educationalists defend the 'child-centred approach'. According to Sir William Taylor – who is the Chairman of the Council for the Accreditation of Teacher Education, which monitors teacher training in England – child-centred education means, 'We start from where the child is, but that does not mean we are content with that. We set the pace, we have objectives and structure.' According to Janet Trotter, the principal of one of the country's largest teacher training colleges in Cheltenham, child-centred teaching does not mean a lack of discipline or leaving children to do as they wish. Rather it means 'ensuring the child develops at what is the appropriate pace for them'.

Mixed ability or streaming?
The other issue that has been given a lot of media attention is whether pupils in any particular age-group should be taught together irrespective of ability or whether they should be grouped by ability within classes or 'streamed' into whole classes based on ability. 'Mixed-ability teaching' is the term given to an approach which does not divide pupils up according to ability. It is very hard to assess how widespread it is. It is certainly a difficult approach to deliver. According to the recently retired Senior Chief Inspector of Schools, Eric Bolton, most teachers could not do it effectively. He believes that the wider the range of ability, the harder it is for teachers to make it work. He says that 'most teachers aim for the middle: the bright children are frustrated and the ones at the bottom get left behind'.

According to Eric Bolton – speaking at the start of the 1990s – most schools no longer do much mixed ability teaching. However the opposite of mixed ability – streaming – is also fairly unusual at primary level. In the 1960s, though, it was the most common way of organising junior schools. Following the famous inquiry into primary education by the Plowden Committee in 1967, streaming began to be discredited on the basis that selection was too often inaccurate at so early an age. Today the more usual practice is for teachers to arrange pupils in ability groups within the class, perhaps in different groups for different activities. Often the children themselves will be unaware that this grouping is taking place. When choosing schools you may want to ask what approach they take.

What are mixed-age classes or 'family grouping'?
This is not to be confused with mixed-ability teaching. It means that the school has decided to cut across the age group when placing children in classes. For example, a class may have children ranging from five to seven. Children will stay in the same class for two years, usually with the same teacher.

For many small schools this is often the only effective way to organise themselves. Others choose to do it because they see advantages for the children, with older childen able to help the younger ones along. For some children being one of the older ones in the class is a great confidence booster. The other side of this is that some five-year-olds can lose confidence when taught alongside seven year-olds. However, children would normally be taught in groups within the class, so reducing the age difference. Mixed-age classes are probably rather more difficult to organise under the National Curriculum than they were before.

What is project or topic work?
Much teaching in primary schools today is based on projects. So, instead of your child coming home and saying they have had lessons in science, history and geography, they are much more likely to tell you (if prompted sufficiently) that they are doing a project on, say, transport or homes. The project is simply a way of covering aspects of several subjects through a particular theme.

The advantages of projects are that they allow lots of practical work and encourage children to find things out for themselves. Many teachers believe 'learning by discovery' is the most effective way to teach young children. Projects also allow teachers to introduce children to aspects of subjects like history or geography before they start to study these subjects in more detail separately at a later stage. However, some educationalists say project work is sometimes too loosely organised. They recommend that projects should be closely tied to just one subject – say history – rather than trying to cover the whole spread of the curriculum through one theme.

■ LEARNING TO READ
The ability to read is an essential key to the rest of learning. It is said by some experts that if a child is not reading well by the age of seven, he or she will probably never fully catch up. However the process of learning to read remains something we still barely understand. There are a number of different approaches to the teaching of reading. These have fallen in and out of fashion. They have also been the subject of one of the fiercest education debates of recent years. It has probably caused more concern amongst parents than any other educational issue.

Newspapers have recently devoted many column inches – and

impassioned editorials – to a method of teaching reading known as 'real books'. It derives its name from the fact that it does not involve the use of books designed for a structured reading scheme or books which have been specially written to encourage the development of certain words or sounds. They are simply 'real' ordinary books, fiction or non-fiction, written for the enjoyment of children. The idea behind the 'real books' approach is that children learn best if they want to read and that happens when they enjoy reading. Supporters of this approach also argue that children who learn this way are better at understanding the meaning of what they are reading, rather than just being able to recognise a string of individual words.

However the 'real books' approach has come under fire. It has been blamed by some for causing a decline in reading standards amongst children. These critics say this approach does not equip children with the tools they need to work out an unfamiliar word. They prefer the 'phonics' approach. This is based on children learning the sounds of individual letters and groups of letters. Supporters of phonics argue that once a child knows the sight and sound of all their letters, then they are equipped to read. Other methods of teaching reading include 'look-and-say' where children learn to recognise whole words by their shape and pattern, and teaching children to compose their own words and sentences from banks of letters and words.

Despite the storm over the 'real books' method, it would appear that only a very small number of schools use this approach on its own. Most schools use a variety of methods, including both 'real books' and phonics. Most also use graded reading schemes. However, parents may want to satisfy themselves where the balance lies at their child's school. School inspectors have recommended that a mix of methods be used and that teachers should not rely on any one approach. They say the different approaches reinforce each other.

Experts also agree it is important that sufficient time is devoted to reading. This is proving difficult as the National Curriculum requires a wider range of subjects to be covered than was usual in primary schools in the past. Inspectors say it is important that teachers hear individual children reading aloud on a regular basis. However they also warn that teachers must beware of the risk of concentrating too heavily on individual work to the extent that their attention is too thinly spread amongst the whole class. Reading is one area where regular voluntary help in the class from parents can be extremely useful.

READING JARGON EXPLAINED

Reading scheme a set of books specifically designed and graded to develop reading skills through which children progress in a structured way. An example is the Oxford Reading Tree.

Home-school partnership an agreed approach between the school and parents for help with reading in the home.

'Real books' method emphasises motivating children by letting them read the books that interest them, rather than books from reading schemes.

Phonics method teaches children to recognise words by sounding out individual letters and combinations of letters. So 'Kuh-ah-tuh' gives you the sounds of 'cat'.

Look-and-say method teaches children to recognise words by their shape and pattern. The Janet and John series of books was based on this method.

While there remains concern that standards are falling – or at least are not rising as fast as they ought to be – that view has not been proven. Changing methods of testing reading ability makes comparisons over the years difficult. Provisional results from the first tests for seven-year-olds in England and Wales suggest that around one in four children failed to reach Level Two in reading, or in other words they were still not reading fluently and independently towards the end of the infant school. While that may suggest cause for concern, there are no comparable tests for previous years so the results cannot indicate whether standards are rising or falling. The recently-published study by Professor Alexander of Leeds University does, however, support claims that standards are falling. Alexander's study of inner city schools in Leeds found a decline in recent years in the reading scores of seven and nine-year-olds.

The search for the cause of unsatisfactory reading standards is also incomplete, although there is now broad agreement that there is no single factor. The widespread use of television, videos and computers in the home nowadays is one possible cause. In the past children may only have read comics with little literary value, but at least they were reading. Now they are more likely to be sitting at a keyboard or joystick. Class sizes, home background, high turnover of teachers, and the pressure of other subjects in the school curriculum could also have an influence.

■ HOW TO HELP YOUR CHILD

Reading is certainly one area where you can greatly assist your child. Inspectors say the quality and extent of parents' support has 'a positive effect on their standards of reading'. As leading reading expert Betty Root puts it, the key to reading 'is an adult who has time and cares. Time is the most important thing you can give to small children and both teachers and parents need to be aware of that.'

You can help your child by keeping books in your home and by taking your child on visits to the library. Try to read with your child, but without making it a chore or something he or she resents. Trying to force a young child to read when tired will be counter-productive. Encourage your child to ask if he or she does not understand a word, but do not stop every time they get a word wrong.

Remember too that children learn by example. If they see you spending most of your spare time in front of the television they are unlikely to be highly motivated to read themselves. Try to make the time you spend reading with your children a special time, when they have your full attention. Reading to them is just as valuable as listening to them read to you. Do both.

Good schools will encourage you to be involved in teaching your child to read. Since this is largely a one-to-one activity, they would be wrong to reject your help. A good school will tell you how they approach the teaching of reading. If they do not, ask them. Almost all schools arrange for children to take books home to read. Some provide a 'home/school contact book'. This is a comment book for you and your child to fill in, saying whether or not your child enjoyed the book and how easy or difficult they found it. Although it can be very hard to find the time, it is important that you do participate. Otherwise your child will note your lack of interest. Most schools will also welcome parents who are willing to come into school to listen to children read.

The help you can give your child goes well beyond reading. The days when some teachers may have regarded education as being a matter for professionals alone are over. Get involved. Show an interest in the work your child is doing at a school. If they are doing a project on – say – local history or transport, you can point out things which are relevant on your walks or car journeys. Always try to answer their questions however much it may try your patience and ingenuity. Questions like 'Why is the sky blue?' can baffle many parents, but if you do not know the answer try to look it up and involve your child in that process.

ONE SCHOOL'S ADVICE TO PARENTS ON READING WITH YOUR CHILD:

- remember the aim is not simply to memorise and repeat a book parrot-fashion.
- discuss the front cover and title of the book.
- ask straightforward questions about the text.
- ask your child to predict what will happen next.
- ask your child to retell the story in their own words.
- ask why they liked or disliked the book.
- discuss punctuation (why we need to pause for a breath; how we know which words are spoken by which characters etc.)

Most ordinary household activities can quite naturally involve elements of learning. Letting your child help with the cooking, for example, can lead to simple science and mathematics involving weighing ingredients and counting out spoonfuls. Many parents are nervous about getting involved in teaching their children to write, fearing they will confuse them if they follow a different method from the school. Once again, the best thing is to find out what approach the school is taking and use that. Encouraging your child to write birthday cards or thankyou letters helps to develop their writing ability. For young children, most activities like this can combine drawing, painting, sticking and cutting-out as well as letter formation. Once again, activities at home should ideally be fun not a chore. This, though, does not rule out setting challenges, such as filling in the missing letter, or more straightforward spelling tests, or even copying out the alphabet or letter shapes. Children often enjoy the discipline of such activities.

3
SECONDARY
SCHOOL
■

HOW TO CHOOSE A SECONDARY SCHOOL

WHAT MAKES A GOOD SCHOOL?

CITY TECHNOLOGY COLLEGES

FEE-CHARGING SCHOOLS

■ HOW TO CHOOSE A SECONDARY SCHOOL

Choosing the right school for your child at 11 is possibly even more important than at five. Many youngsters are turned off education in their early teens, just when it is important that they do their best in preparation for examinations. Discipline problems are likely to be more of an issue at secondary school and the availability of resources for specialist subjects like science or technology becomes of greater importance.

As with primary schools, though, it is still a matter of choosing the right school for your child. By this stage, parents should have a much clearer idea of the strengths and weaknesses of their children. They may have a better idea whether their child is suited to an ordered, disciplined atmosphere or a more relaxed, informal approach. They may already be showing a particular leaning towards science or music and parents may want to choose a school that is strong in that area. There may well be a choice of different types of school, and parents need to think about the sort of subject choices their child may wish to make at a later stage in their schooling. It is also important to think ahead and take into account whether or not the school has its own sixth-form or whether it feeds into a separate sixth-form college or tertiary college.

QUESTIONS TO ASK YOURSELF BEFORE CHOOSING SCHOOLS
- What are my aims for my children?
- What are their aims/interests/abilities?
- Will they benefit from academically selective schooling?
- Are they bright enough to pass entrance examinations?
- Do they have special educational needs?
- What sort of working environment suits them?
- Would they be better in a single-sex or a co-educational school?
- Do they react better to a disciplined or more relaxed approach?
- How far is it reasonable for them to travel each day?
- Are they likely to want to stay in school (rather than college) after 16?
- Do I want them to wear uniform?

The next step is to find out what is available. As with primary schools, you can obtain a list of state secondary schools in your area from your local education authority. You should also consider writing to neighbouring education authorities if you are within travelling distance of their schools. Do not forget to find out whether there are any City Technology Colleges or Grant Maintained Schools in your area. You may also wish to consider local independent secondary schools or – if you wish your child to be a boarder – you can look as far afield as you wish. However if you are considering paying for your child's education, it is worth visiting your local state schools before taking a final decision to take out a second mortgage.

Even if you are unhappy with your local schools, travel costs to a more distant state school will be much cheaper than paying school fees. Many parents opt for independent education on purely anecdotal evidence that state schools are not very good. Often this considered advice has come from other parents of children at fee-charging schools who are anxious to justify (to themselves as much as anyone else) their decision to fork out large amounts each term. So do not assume that your child will get a better education simply because you are paying for it. Sometimes they will, sometimes they will not.

The lists on the right are not exhaustive. There are bound to be other questions arising and other things you will notice when visiting schools. However, here is a word of caution on how you compare schools based on the information you have gained. Examination results need to be treated with care. Overall pass rates do, of course,

WHAT TO LOOK FOR IN A SECONDARY SCHOOL
- are pupils polite, friendly and helpful to visitors?
- is there an atmosphere of learning?
- how do pupils behave in classrooms, corridors and elsewhere?
- what is the physical state of the classrooms, desks, toilets?
- is there much rubbish or graffiti?
- how do pupils and staff relate to each other?
- look at noticeboards to see the extent of activities.
- look at display boards: what range of successes is celebrated?
- check to see how well-stocked and well-used the library is.
- are classrooms over-crowded?
- look at the amount and quality of specialist equipment for science, technology, art, music, drama and sport.

QUESTIONS TO ASK ABOUT SECONDARY SCHOOLS
- what are the school's aims?
- how big are the classes?
- are classes mixed-ability or streamed?
- which subjects are offered in addition to the National Curriculum?
- are there limits on the combinations of subjects pupils can take?
- does the school offer a range of courses leading to vocational qualifications?
- what is the homework policy?
- what is the school's examinations record?
- what proportion of pupils stay on at school after 16?
- how many are there in the sixth-form?
- what do pupils do when they leave?
- what is the school's policy on discipline?
- which extra-curricular activities are offered?
- is the turnover of staff high?
- are most subjects taught by staff who trained in that discipline?
- what is the school's long-term future: is it likely to merge with another, change its status, or opt out?

tell you something. But they can be misleading if schools do not enter pupils for examinations in which they think they may score poorly. You must also take into account how examination results at one school compare with another in a similar catchment area. Schools have only recently been required to publish all results in a consistent form to allow parents to make meaningful comparisons between schools. As with all statistics it is important to compare like with like. A grammar school in a middle-class area would expect to get very good examination results, but it may be that a non-selective school in a less up-market area has actually done more to raise the achievement levels of its pupils than its absolute scores would suggest. Naturally parents will want their child to be educated alongside other bright children, but you must think hard about what a school will do for your individual child rather than its overall examination successes.

WHAT SCHOOLS MUST TELL YOU ABOUT EXAMINATION RESULTS

- GCSE, A and A/S Level and vocational qualification results must be published in full.
- results must be published in a consistent format each year with a comparison with the previous year.
- comparison must be made with average figures for the local education authority and for the whole country.
- figures must show: the number of pupils in year groups; the number entered for examinations; the number achieving each grade and failing to achieve a pass grade.
- separate figures must be given for boys and girls to allow parents to assess their relative performance.
- percentage pass/fail rates must be based on the total number of pupils in that age group, not just those entered for the examinations.

Similar caution should be taken when considering the quality of buildings and equipment. Of course, as a parent you want your child to have the very best that is available. But the quality of the teaching is more important, and there may be schools with excellent teachers and poor facilities. The long-term future of the school is also an important issue. Often change cannot be predicted, but if there are declining pupil numbers in your area there is always the possibility that schools will merge or even close. While this may not be a bad thing in itself, it could be very disruptive for your child if it comes at a crucial point in his or her school career. Merger proposals do not usually come out of the blue, so it is worth asking if any such suggestions have been aired locally.

■ WHAT MAKES A GOOD SCHOOL?

There is no magic formula for a good school. So the most important thing is to go and see for yourself and trust your own judgment, rather than second-hand hearsay. Nevertheless it is useful to know what the experts say. A 1989 study of comprehensives, *The School Effect* by David J. Smith and Sally Tomlinson (Policy Studies Institute), argued that the same child would get markedly different examination scores at different schools. The study – carried out on 3000 pupils in 20 urban comprehensive schools – found that while the child might get a good O Level pass at one school, he or she would fail at another. (The actual comparison, made before the introduction of the GCSE, was between a B grade O Level and a grade 3 CSE.) The study concluded that this difference would apply across all subjects, but was unable to say why schools differed so much. However, an earlier study – *Fifteen Thousand Hours* by Michael Rutter (Open Books 1979) – did find some common characteristics amongst effective schools. These included:

★ teachers prepared lessons in advance and directed their attention to the class as a whole rather than to groups doing different activities.

★ teachers arrived on time for classes.

★ teachers expressed high expectations of pupils.

★ homework was regularly set and marked.

★ the school was well led from the top, but all staff had a chance to contribute their views in the running of the school.

★ pupils worked in pleasant conditions.

★ teachers gave ample praise to pupils and disciplinary interventions were few, but firm.

★ approaches to discipline and the curriculum were agreed and supported by the whole staff acting together.

★ staff and pupils engaged in joint out-of-school activities.

★ pupils were given posts of responsibility (eg form captain, prefect).

One final point is that you should consider your child's own views. In this respect, choosing a secondary school is different from selecting a primary school. There may be factors you have overlooked. A soccer-mad boy may be very upset if you choose a school where they only play rugby. Some children may strongly resent the idea of wearing a uniform. The changeover from primary to secondary school is very traumatic for most children. They are parted from friends and often have to travel long distances from home to school. The scale of most secondary schools is vast compared to primaries. It may well be the biggest change so far in their lives.

■ CITY TECHNOLOGY COLLEGES

One new type of non-fee-charging school that parents may wish to consider is the City Technology College, or CTC. These were launched in 1986 to act as 'beacons of excellence' turning out highly motivated youngsters with the scientific and technological skills that the economy required. The original plan was for 20 new colleges to be paid for mainly by industrial and business sponsors, with the running costs coming from central government. The plan was a revolutionary concept in British education history. After a slow start, the Government decided to allow existing schools to become CTCs through the opting-out process.

The models for the CTCs were the American 'magnet' schools, which specialise in different subject areas. CTCs usually emphasise scientific and technological skills. Some cover the performing arts and their associated technologies (theatre lighting, sound recording etc.). They also specifically prepare pupils for the world of work. They are mainly in inner city areas, where ministers felt existing schools were not doing well. CTCs are independent of local education authorities and are run by their own governing bodies, which include representatives of the main industrial sponsors.

A CITY TECHNOLOGY COLLEGE
- is a non-profit-making independent school.
- does not charge pupils fees.
- is owned and run by a 'promoter' but receives running costs from government.
- places special emphasis on science and technology or the technology of arts.
- is usually located in a disadvantaged inner city area.
- caters for 11 to 18-year-olds of all abilities.

CTCs are intended to select pupils by aptitude rather than by ability. The overall aim is to provide equal access to boys and girls, although individual single-sex CTCs are not ruled out. Selection is undertaken by the head teacher and the Governing Body, taking into account applicants' achievements at primary school, their aptitude and readiness for the particular type of curriculum, and their parents' commitment to full-time education up to 18. Individual companies, educational trusts, charities and other voluntary organisations are the expected 'promoters' of CTCs. These promoters are expected to meet the costs of the buildings and equipment and to contribute a substantial amount of the running costs of the schools.

What will children learn at CTCs?

Although CTCs specialise in specific areas of the curriculum, they are required to offer a broad-based education. So the extra emphasis on technological and vocational skills comes on top of the national curriculum, not instead of it. The approach builds on an earlier government scheme – now available in most ordinary schools – known as the Technical and Vocational Education Initiative (TVEI). It aims to prepare pupils for adult life, including employment and the responsibilities of citizenship. It involves a practical approach to subjects, with emphasis as much on doing and making as on knowing.

The Department of Education suggested a number of model timetables for CTCs. For example, pupils from age 11 to 14 might have their time split as follows:

★ 25 per cent humanities, including English, history, geography and RE.

★ 25 per cent mathematics and science, including some aspects of technology.

★ 20 per cent design and its realisation.

★ 30 per cent other courses, including modern languages, expressive arts, and PE/games.

Older pupils – from 14 to 16 – would be given rather more choice of subject. For them a typical timetable might look like this:

★ 20 per cent science, either as separate subjects or integrated.

★ 10 per cent mathematics.

★ 10 per cent design and technology, including art, computing, information technology.

★ 10 per cent understanding industry.

★ 10 per cent English.

★ 10 per cent modern languages.

★ 10 per cent RE/personal development and PE/games.

★ 10 per cent humanities option such as economics, history or geography.

★ 10 per cent 'open' option from wide range of subjects in which school has strengths.

After 16, more flexibility is introduced with one or two-year courses available, leading to a range of qualifications. All students would follow general studies, careers and recreational courses. In addition they could choose from the following combinations of

courses (more details are given in the chapter 'Choices At Sixteen'):
★ one year courses leading to Royal Society of Arts, Certificate of Pre-Vocational Education or GCSE qualifications.
★ one or two-year vocational courses leading to Business and Technology Education Council (BTEC) or City and Guilds qualifications.
★ two-year courses leading to GCE A levels or A/S levels.
★ a mixture of any of the above.
★ two-year courses leading to the International Baccalaureate.

In practice, the exact nature of what is on offer will vary from one CTC to another, according to its chosen area of expertise. However, it is not only what they teach which makes CTCs different from other schools. They have also tended to operate longer school days and longer terms, and the atmosphere is very different too. In those CTCs which have been purpose-built there is lavish and expensive provision for all pupils and an atmosphere of pioneering experimentation. The contrast to the surrounding location is often stark. The Djanogly City Technology College in Nottingham is fairly typical.

A City Technology College profile: Djanogly CTC
The Djanogly CTC is close to Nottingham city centre in a rather nondescript area off the Mansfield Road. It was one of the first purpose-built CTCs and does not look much like a school at all: the resemblance is more to a modern, hi-tech office block. It has the sort of reception area you expect to encounter at an airport check-in. It is carpeted and softly lit throughout and has more computer screens than an electrical superstore. Before it opened, a glossy brochure with a pre-paid business reply card was sent to parents in the area. On its opening day – in September 1989 – the first batch of pupils were clearly impressed with what they saw, including space-age language laboratories and a 'Faculty of Expressive Arts'.

Djanogly CTC is named after a local industrialist who donated £1 million to the school. Other sponsors included Boots, W.H. Smith, and Marks and Spencer. Total sponsorship was £1.88 million. However the total cost of creating the college was £9.75 million. Like other CTCs, Djanogly operates a longer than usual school day. Pupils attend from 8.00 am to 3.30 pm when they are 11 and 12. At 13 and 14 they stay later, until 4.30 pm and from 15 they stay until 5.30 pm. The usual three-term year is changed to four terms, each ten weeks long with no half-term holidays. The CTC academic year lasts around 200 days, compared to 190 in maintained schools.

Supporters of CTCs say that on average the colleges provide formal lessons for at least 25 hours a week, usually on the basis of 36 lessons of 45 minutes each. On top of this there are usually at least six further hours of activities such a drama, music, remedial work, sports and school societies. In mainstream secondary schools it has been estimated that almost half of all schools provide just 23 hours of formal lessons a week.

In the first three years at Djanogly, pupils will devote 50 per cent of their formal classroom time to mathematics, science and technology. In the fourth and fifth years, this will increase to 60 per cent. The college says it will also encourage 'personal development, an understanding of wealth creation, and a positive attitude towards industry and business' throughout pupils' time there. The school itself is divided into four faculties:

Science, Mathematics and Technology
– this includes electronics, manufacture and computer-aided design.

Expressive Arts
– covers the main arts subjects, including singing, instrument practice, modelling, graphics, drama, PE and games. Home economics – which includes home design and child care – is also covered by this faculty.

Heritage and Communications
– covers history, geography and economics as part of the aim of understanding historical and political development both locally and internationally. Communications covers English, foreign languages and information technology.

Student Services and Business Links
– this part of the college has strong links with outside businesses and prepares pupils for working life.

Students at Djanogly will all spend equal time on the following core subjects: English, mathematics, science, technology, a modern language, business studies, physical education, and religious education. They will work towards GCSE qualifications at 16. After that, they can work towards the more traditional A and A/S levels and towards vocational qualifications such as the Certificate of Pre-vocational Education, BTEC (Business and Technology Education Council) Diplomas, and Youth Training Schemes.

The future for CTCs

Although some £35 million was raised from private sponsors for the first 15 CTCs, the taxpayer was left with the bulk of the cost. It became clear that the Treasury was not willing to continue on this basis. So plans are being worked on for new types of CTCs, using existing schools either run in partnership with local education authorities or as Grant Maintained schools. Much will depend on the future shape of politics, since both the Labour Party and the Liberal Democrats are very cool about CTCs and have said they will bring them back under the control of education authorities.

■ FEE-CHARGING SCHOOLS

There is a tremendous variety of fee-charging schools. They are sometimes described as 'private' schools. But although some are privately-owned and run for profit, the larger, better-known schools are charitable foundations. Taken as a whole this sector of education is thriving, although some areas are suffering declining popularity. The proportion of the school age population at fee-charging schools has risen steadily over the past decade from below 6 per cent in the late 1970s to just under 7.5 per cent at the start of the 1990s. Around one in five sixth-formers are in independent schools. The current trend is one of increasing popularity for day-schools and weekly boarding, with a decline in the more traditional termly boarding. There have also been higher than average increases in the number of girls and under-fives of both sexes at fee-charging schools.

The best source of information on the main independent schools is the Independent Schools Information Service. ISIS can be contacted at: 56 Buckingham Gate, London SW1E 6AG, Tel: 071–630–8793/4.

What does it cost?

The cost of sending your child to a fee-charging school has been rising faster than inflation in recent years. At the top end – Cheltenham Ladies', Eton, Harrow, Roedean – senior school boarding fees are around £10,000 a year and rising. Less expensive boarding schools charge upwards of £6000 a year. Fees for day pupils at senior schools range from around £3000 to £8000 a year. These rates are for 1991/2 and, if past trends continue, are likely to go up by around 10 per cent a year. As with preparatory schools, it is worth noting that these are only the basic fees. Schools will charge for many 'extras'.

Find out about these charges when selecting a school. Most parents will only be able to meet these levels of fees if they have planned ahead and taken out insurance policies. There are several specialist school fees financial advisers.

Financial help may be available in the form of scholarships and bursaries provided by the schools themselves. The other main source of help with fees is the government's Assisted Places Scheme established by the 1980 Education Act. It applies to day pupils of 11 and over. The Department of Education or ISIS can provide details of which schools operate the scheme. This scheme is intended to give bright children from less well-off families the opportunity to attend fee-charging schools. Around 300 schools participate in the scheme, but it will not necessarily continue on the same basis if there is a change of government. Grants are based on a means test. Figures change each year, but as a general guide a family earning less than around £9000 a year could be entitled to full fees. That ceiling will be higher if there are several children in the family. Above that level the amount of help decreases in inverse proportion to the family's income.

The Ministry of Defence provides grants to children of parents in the Armed Forces. Some local education authorities will – in exceptional circumstances – give grants to enable children to go to boarding schools. This usually only applies where parents are living abroad or children have special handicaps or abilities.

How to get in

For entrance at 11 or 13, schools will usually require applicants to sit an examination. This may be the school's own examination or – more usually – the Common Entrance Examination. Although set centrally, this exam is marked by the individual school which sets its own pass mark. For entry at 11, there are papers in English, mathematics and verbal reasoning. For entry at 13, the examination consists of papers in English, mathematics, French, science, history, geography and religious education. The Common Entrance Examination is held in February, June and November. Details can be obtained from: Common Entrance Board, Ashley Lane, Lymington, Hampshire, SO41 9YR.

Children at preparatory schools are likely to have an advantage over primary school pupils in the Common Entrance Examination (although a good independent secondary school should take this into account). This is because much of the last two years at preparatory schools is spent specifically preparing for it. Special coaching may be advisable for children outside the independent sector, just to level the playing-field. However many independent secondary schools do not require entrants to take the Common Entrance. It is certainly not essential to go to preparatory school in order to get into independent secondary education. Schools with good academic reputations such as Dulwich College or Manchester Grammar School take almost 70 per cent of their intake from state primary schools. At Eton the figure is just 1 per cent. A recent survey showed that, overall, 44 per cent of new pupils at independent senior schools came from state primary schools.

Why choose a fee-charging school?
The same arguments apply here as for junior schools. However there is one important difference, namely that fee-charging senior schools sell themelves to a large extent on the basis of their examination results. These can be very misleading. For example, pass rates may not include pupils who were not put in for the examination. Like all statistics, they can be very flexible. State schools are now required to publish their examination results in a standardised way to enable comparison between schools. You should check the basis on which independent schools publish their results.

In 1991 a number of newspapers began to publish league tables of examination results at independent and state schools. This caused a great flurry in the chicken coop, particularly when state schools were placed higher than some very expensive independent schools. It was claimed, with some justification, that these league tables were unfair. However it is worth recalling that many independent schools have in the past based their reputations largely on academic success.

Comparisons are unfair because most independent schools are highly selective. If they take only the brightest pupils, then there would be something very wrong if they were not getting the best results. Equally, though, many of the state grammar schools are even more selective than top independent schools. Nevertheless, the reality is that some comprehensives – taking the whole ability range – scored better in these league tables than many of the grandest independent schools.

In the end, though, these national league tables – although clearly here to stay – are of relatively little value for parents choosing a school in their locality. Moreover, what counts is how well a school will educate your child rather than how high its examination scores are. This involves a more sophisticated judgement comparing examination results with the abilities of pupils on entry to the school. And – as independent as well as state school head teachers will tell you – examination results are but one amongst many factors which determine a good school.

What other factors persuade parents to choose fee-charging schools? According to ISIS, parents look beyond the state sector for smaller classes, traditional values, strong discipline, and good facilities for sport, art, music and drama.

Boarding

Many parents also prefer a boarding school education for their children. This has the advantage of giving parents a much wider geographical choice of schools. Supporters of boarding say it encourages independence and a more adult approach to life while also ensuring the discipline of enforced 'prep' or homework each evening away from the temptations of the local youth club or television. There are also greater opportunities for after-school clubs, societies, and sport. There are a few boarding schools in the state sector, but most of the 120,000 boarders in Britain are at independent schools.

The traditional, spartan image of boarding schools has changed. Many are now co-educational, particularly in the sixth-form. Mill Hill school is typical of the way boarding schools are changing. Set in 120 acres of north London hillside, its head master Alistair Graham can boast of having 'five pupils per acre'. At around £10,000 a year each, boarders make an interesting cash crop! The school is gradually getting rid of its large dormitories and replacing them with comfortable, carpeted rooms. Younger pupils are four to a room, older pupils share with one other and sixth-formers can have a study/bedroom of their own. All boarders are allowed home for Saturday night. The boarding houses have common rooms with pool and billiard tables. Nevertheless it is not all play. There are lengthy periods of prep in the evening and lessons on Saturday morning.

However, rising fees and changing fashions – and perhaps also some well-publicised incidents of sexual abuse and bullying at boarding schools – have combined to produce a steady decline in boarding. More and more schools are now offering weekly boarding, where pupils can come home at weekends. However – unless the decline is reversed –many rural boarding schools face a difficult future, since they do not have the local population to replace full boarders with either weekly boarders or day pupils.

4
THE
NATIONAL
CURRICULUM
■

WHAT IS THE NATIONAL CURRICULUM?
WHAT WILL YOUR CHILD HAVE TO STUDY?
HOW HAS IT CHANGED TEACHING?

■ WHAT IS THE NATIONAL CURRICULUM?

For the first time ever in England and Wales, schools must now teach a curriculum set down by the government. Schools have already been told which subjects they must teach and what topics within them must be covered. However, in order to give schools time to adapt to the changes, the new curriculum is being introduced gradually and will not be fully in place for all pupils until 1996 (see table on page 199).

The National Curriculum is compulsory for all state schools and for virtually all pupils from five to 16. The only exception will be for some children who have special educational needs. Although it has taken a long time to introduce a National Curriculum – something that has been common elsewhere in Europe for years – it is here to stay. Past resistance has melted away and the principle, if not the precise form, is now widely accepted by teachers and politicians of all the main parties.

The main aim of the National Curriculum is to raise standards, making sure all children have a broad and balanced education right up to 16. In the past, many pupils dropped key subjects like modern languages or science at 13 or 14. A second aim is to ensure that schools in all parts of the country are following the same courses.

THE NATIONAL CURRICULUM
- makes certain subjects compulsory for almost all children from five to 16.
- lays down what they must be taught within those subjects.
- sets out what children are expected to know at different ages.

This has particular advantages for children who change school when families move house from one area to another. It also means that your child's progress through a particular subject is clearly mapped out. This should ensure that in history, for example, pupils do not study the Vikings three times in their school career without ever covering the Norman Conquest. In the past this could happen.

The National Curriculum specifies what children must study and what they are expected to know at different ages. This ties in with the new national tests which will check whether your child is meeting these targets. The detailed content of courses is devised by experts chosen by the Education Secretary, although he or she takes the final decision. These decisions can be changed by future Education Secretaries, but whatever happens politically, the National Curriculum is unlikely to change much in the next few years, as schools are still only just getting used to it.

What about independent schools?
Independent schools do not have to teach the National Curriculum, although the Labour Party has said it will require them to do so. In fact, many independent schools are already following all or most of the new curriculum. They say it reflects the broad and balanced curriculum they have always advocated. Also they realise it will be very difficult to stand apart.

Text books and educational materials will be adapted to the new curriculum. More significantly, the national system of examinations at 16 – the GCSE – is being brought into line with it. Parents who are paying fees will not expect to be sold short and will want to make comparisons between national test results in independent schools and in state schools. Also independent schools will not wish to make it more difficult than at present for children to transfer to them from state schools.

Adapting to the National Curriculum should not involve great problems for the bigger, more established independent schools.

Many of these will – like state grammar schools – continue to offer extra subjects to more able pupils. But since a broad curriculum and regular testing are very much in tune with the independent school approach, they will readily adapt to it. Only a few of the most traditionalist schools are likely to resist the National Curriculum. Some of the smaller preparatory schools – with relatively few teachers – may find it difficult to broaden their approach. However, the bigger preparatory schools will continue to offer a foreign language, something which is not required in primary school.

■ WHAT YOUR CHILD MUST STUDY

The core subjects of the new curriculum are English, mathematics and science. In Welsh-speaking schools in Wales, the Welsh language is an extra core subject. These are the most important school subjects and are compulsory for all pupils right through until 16, with virtually all youngsters required to take a GCSE at the end of their courses.

The second level of the new curriculum is made up of seven so-called foundation subjects: history, geography, technology, a modern foreign language, music, art, and physical education. In English-speaking schools in Wales, the Welsh language is an extra foundation subject. All of these subjects – except a foreign language – must be taught through primary school. In secondary school they must all be taught to pupils up to 14. In addition, Religious Education is a compulsory subject at all ages although it is not part of the National Curriculum.

Originally all National Curriculum subjects were to be compulsory until 16. But it became clear that this would overload timetables and squeeze out extra subjects like classics, economics or a second foreign language. Also many pupils simply could not manage ten subjects at GCSE. So it has been decided that some foundation subjects can now be dropped by pupils at 14. So alongside English, mathematics and science, all pupils must be taught technology, a foreign language and physical education right through until 16. However unlike the three core subjects, pupils are not required to take a GCSE in these subjects. In addition to these six compulsory subjects, all pupils must take either history or geography – or a course combining one of them with another subject – until 16. Unless the government changes its mind, music and art can be dropped at 14.

So the National Curriculum subjects look like this:

WHO MUST STUDY WHAT?
5 to 11 English, mathematics, science, technology, geography, history, music, art, PE.
11 to 14 all the above plus a modern foreign language.
14 to 16 English, mathematics and science compulsory to GCSE. Technology, a modern foreign language, and PE must be studied. Either History or Geography or a combined course must be studied. Music and art are optional.

■ HOW HAS IT AFFECTED TEACHING?

Opinions vary on the effects of the new curriculum on teaching in schools. Many teachers say it only represents what they have always done. But there have been changes. For a start, all teachers have had to reassess the way they have been teaching to ensure that they are fulfilling the new requirements of the National Curriculum. But the new requirement to teach certain compulsory subjects has certainly brought change, particularly in primary schools.

Primary Schools

Since the demise of the 11+ examination in most areas, primary schools have not been affected by national tests or examinations, so they had almost complete freedom over what and how they taught. Now that is changing. Of course all primary schools taught English and mathematics, but many did very little science, history, or technology. Now they must cover nine compulsory subjects. This is particularly difficult for primary teachers who – unlike secondary school subject specialists – usually take one class for all subjects. Now, whether or not they have the appropriate expertise, they must, for example, teach science. As Chris Thornhill, head teacher of Plymtree Primary in Devon says, 'There are teachers who have no experience of the greater depths of science or who have no real background in history and who will be expected to teach things that are beyond their knowledge.'

To overcome teachers' lack of expertise in science, many schools have appointed one member of staff to be a science co-ordinator. This person will go on courses and study the science curriculum in detail and then share their new expertise with colleagues. The arrival of the National Curriculum has encouraged most primary schools to appoint such co-ordinators for each of the main areas of the new curriculum. So, if you have particular concerns about the way a subject is being taught, then – after speaking to your child's own teacher – you could ask to speak to the relevant subject co-ordinator.

One recent survey found that schools are now doing more planning and more precise record-keeping and that teachers are increasingly pooling their expertise. It found that teachers' main concerns were that the new curriculum had been introduced too quickly and that it had dramatically increased their workload. School inspectors' reports on the introduction of the new curriculum in primary schools have also found that teachers' preparation has improved and that the new curriculum has highlighted a shortage of resources and equipment in many schools.

Small primary schools – particularly those with fewer than 100 children – face the biggest difficulties with the new curriculum. They usually have less equipment and fewer teachers, making it harder to achieve a range of subject specialism across the school. Supporters of small schools fear that the National Curriculum will be used as an excuse for closures and mergers. They argue that small schools can overcome these difficulties if neighbouring schools pool their resources. For example, four small village schools in Suffolk have formed themselves into the 'Felixstowe Peninsula Federation' to share equipment, teachers and expertise. The teachers move between the four schools, teaching pupils and sharing ideas with other staff. They sometimes even bring children from all the schools together for combined classes. Supporters of small schools also believe that any disadvantages are offset by the advantages of smaller classes and their more human scale.

Most primary schools have stayed with the now common practice of teaching more than one subject at a time through project or topic work. Although some schools might have single subject lessons in English, mathematics and science, it is more common for several aspects of the curriculum to be covered under the umbrella of a particular theme. So, for example, a topic on conservation might cover aspects of science and geography while also including skills in mathematics (collecting and recording data, for example) and English (writing up their findings).

Topic work is not new in primary schools. But it has sometimes been alleged that this approach is not always clearly focused. Now teachers are having to reappraise topics to make sure they do cover all the necessary parts of the new curriculum. Parents might wonder why their child does not appear to be having lessons on geography or history when these are compulsory subjects. However it is likely that these subjects are being covered through topic or project work.

For example, at Bare Trees primary school in Oldham infants have been doing a project on fruit. They visited their local market, where they bought apples, bananas, oranges and so on from the stall-holders. Working out how much things would cost, tendering the correct money and checking their change provided useful number work for their mathematics. They then brought the fruit back to their classroom where they dissected it, looking at seeds, pips and stones. This involved some simple science. They also did some weighing experiments, seeing which fruits were heavier than others. Once again, this covered areas of science and mathematics.

In theory, the same topic could be used to cover geography (where different fruits are grown and how they are transported) or history (how our diet has changed over the years). Similarly, music could be included through songs about fruit, art through drawing or painting pictures, and English through learning to spell and writing out the names of fruit and describing other aspects of the project. All this, though, takes a lot of planning if the teacher is to ensure that the right parts of each of these subjects are being covered in accordance with the National Curriculum.

Topic work does not always attempt to cover the whole range of the National Curriculum. Sometimes projects or activities revolve around one subject. Indeed inspectors have said that some subjects – like geography and history – are usually better approached through topics which are based on those individual subjects. Some activities are designed by schools to cover several of the new curriculum requirements for one subject. Linda Pagett, a teacher at Plymtree Primary, set up a mock café in her classroom as part of English lessons. The children take the parts of both waiters and customers. By reading and writing menus and giving and taking orders, the children can cover the main areas of the English curriculum: speaking and listening, reading and writing.

Although topic and project work will continue, the National Curriculum looks like bringing greater change at the top end of primary schools, particularly for nine to 11-year-olds. This may be a good thing according to school inspectors who have been saying for some time that many schools fail to stretch children at this age. Larger schools – with a greater range of staff expertise – may eventually move more towards the secondary school practice of specialist teachers and separate lessons for separate subjects.

Overall, the new curriculum means parents can be assured that their children will be getting a broad education wherever they are at school. The nine National Curriculum subjects must be covered. If you fear they are not, then speak to the class teacher or head teacher. It may be that your child does not realise they are being taught geography, for example, even though the subject is being covered through topic work.

However many parents may be concerned that this new requirement for breadth in the timetable may lead to less concentration on basic subjects. Certainly many primary teachers are concerned that the requirement to teach subjects like technology, geography and history will leave less time for reading, writing and mathematics. However the law does not lay down how much time should be given to each of the compulsory subjects. So, if you are concerned about the emphasis being given to reading, for example, then let the school know.

Secondary Schools

While secondary schools may not feel the impact of the new curriculum quite so sharply as primary schools, they have had to change too. When it was first being introduced, the new change was described as 'very rapid' by Richard Tanner, head teacher of The Vyne school, Basingstoke. He added that in all his time in teaching he had 'never known of anything so fast or as far-reaching'. The biggest challenge for school timetables is to provide the compulsory subjects for all pupils, without losing the flexibility to offer additional subjects. Far more pupils will now continue for longer with subjects like science, foreign languages, history and geography. Even with the less rigid requirements after 14, this leaves relatively little space for optional subjects.

According to Richard Tanner the sort of subjects that could get squeezed out are a second or third modern language, economics, and what is known as Personal and Social Education, which encourages individual development and preparation for adult life. Some grammar schools are finding it hard to find space in the timetable to continue Latin and Greek. For parents, though, the benefit is that it is now clear what your child should be studying. Also, unlike in primary school, it will be easier to see exactly how much time is being given to each subject as they will usually appear separately on the timetable.

Perhaps the obvious change from the sort of timetable most parents will recall is the apparent disappearance of chemistry, physics and biology. Do not worry. These subjects have not been abandoned. Instead they are all included in what is being called *'balanced science'*. The aim is to ensure youngsters follow a broad science education right through to 16. In the past, many pupils have given up one or two of the sciences very early in their career simply because of the heavy workload of three separate subjects. Girls in particular often took only biology.

'Balanced science' is, in effect, a double subject. It will take up about one-fifth of pupils' time in the secondary school and will be worth two GCSEs. Pupils who cannot manage double science – or whose interests lie elsewhere – can take a narrower course leading to a single GCSE. However this will still embrace aspects of all three separate sciences.

Many independent schools are not happy about fitting the three separate sciences into a combined approach. In response to pressure from them, the government decided that all schools can still offer separate sciences at GCSE if they wish. However, the two main head teachers' associations have supported the new balanced science, saying it 'covers all the essential knowledge and concepts contained in the separate sciences and more'.

SCIENCE OPTIONS IN THE NATIONAL CURRICULUM

	Proportion of timetable
Single science	about 12.5 per cent
Double science	about 20 per cent
Separate sciences	about 30 per cent

Another big change for schools is the requirement for pupils to study a *modern foreign language* until 16. In the past around half of all youngsters have given up foreign languages at 14. The most common language is French, but the National Curriculum allows pupils to choose from several languages. These include the eight working languages of the European Community and eleven other languages of commercial and cultural importance (such as Arabic, Hindi, Japanese, Hebrew and Urdu). All schools must offer at least one European language.

In practice, most schools will only be able to offer a very limited range of languages. Nevertheless, more unusual languages have now been given a stamp of approval and more schools may follow the lead of one Berkshire comprehensive which now offers Mandarin

Chinese as a mainstream language for 13-year-olds upwards. Certainly German and Spanish are increasingly popular alternatives to French.

The language requirement will be particularly difficult for teachers to meet because of the current shortage of foreign language teachers. According to the expert committee which drew up the curriculum an extra 1750 teachers will be needed. When choosing a secondary school, parents should ask about the number of language teachers at the school and the range of languages they offer.

Many language teachers regret that the National Curriculum does not require a foreign language in primary school. Hilary Burson, Head of Languages at Burlington Danes School, a comprehensive in west London, says 11-year-olds 'just seem to absorb language like a sponge and if they could start earlier, it would be all to the better'. That view is supported by David Hart of the National Association of Head Teachers who points out that 'most European countries teach their children a foreign language from a much earlier age as too does the independent sector here, and I do not see why the state sector should be deprived of modern language teaching in primary schools'.

Technology is a subject which will be unfamiliar to most parents. It is an entirely new approach, although there are elements of more familiar subjects within it, such as craft-work, business studies, design, and the use of computers including information technology. The subject aims to teach pupils to work out solutions to a whole range of problems which they might encounter in the home, school, workplace or in the wider community. So in the primary school, for example, they might learn how to redesign the layout of their classroom. This could involve devising questionnaires to find out the views of other pupils, using a computer to store the results, and making a model with which to try out different seating plans. In a secondary school, pupils might be asked to analyse, and suggest improvements to, a supermarket check-out system or a local traffic scheme.

The National Curriculum has given a new twist to both *geography* and *history*. In recent years, these have often been combined into social studies or humanities courses. Some experts said this led to important aspects of each subject being ignored. The new curriculum has given them a new lease of life as separate subjects. However – to ease the overcrowding of the timetable – it has been decided that pupils can drop one of the two subjects after 14 or they can follow a shorter course in both subjects leading to a joint history/geography GCSE. It will also be possible to combine short courses in history or geography with other subjects – such as French or business studies – provided pupils study both history and geography. These combined courses will probably lead to either a GCSE or an equivalent vocational qualification, although this has not yet been finalised.

HISTORY AND GEOGRAPHY OPTIONS
As a minimum pupils must study one of the following:
● full history – no geography
● full geography – no history
● short geography **and** short history
● short courses in **both** combined with other subjects e.g. geography/tourism and history/French

---

After a big row over how geography and history should be taught, there has been a slight shift back towards the more traditional approach which emphasises the central place of factual knowledge, with pupils expected to know the names of rivers and mountain ranges or the dates of battles and treaties. This is in opposition to the trend of the GCSE which – with its emphasis on project work – has put greater emphasis on the development of skills of historical and geographical inquiry. This involves the ability to interpret factual material, to weigh evidence and sources, and to 'read' maps and original documents. Of course, both factual content and skills have gone together and one approach does not exclude the other. Indeed, despite this change the National Curriculum still sets great store by the development of skills.

The overall effect the National Curriculum will have on secondary schools is still hard to assess. However according to the 1991 annual report from the Senior Chief Inspector of Schools there were already signs that it was forcing other subjects – like sociology or classics – into retreat. The report also warned that almost three-quarters of schools had inadequate facilities, particularly laboratories, to teach National Curriculum science and technology.

A majority of teachers believe the new curriculum will help break down the traditional picture of girls being drawn to one set of subjects and boys to another. Surveys have suggested that even in the primary school, children tend to follow gender stereotypes when choosing topics or activities. Now boys and girls must do the same things. In secondary school, compulsory 'balanced science' will erode the tendency for boys to opt for physics and girls for biology. Also by ensuring that no youngster abandons science before 16, it is hoped that the National Curriculum will reverse the declining popularity of science amongst sixth-formers.

Finally, despite all the fuss over its introduction, it is now clear that the National Curriculum is here to stay. All the political parties – and most teachers – now regard it as a good thing. That is not to say it is set in concrete. It will be kept under review and arguments will continue over whether, for example, it is right to require only one foreign language or to allow pupils to drop art and music at 14. There will also be pressure to allow secondary school history to cover contemporary events rather than being cut off in the 1960s. But once it is firmly bedded down in schools, there is every sign that it will help to raise standards.

5
TESTS AND
EXAMINATIONS
■

WHY WILL MY CHILD BE TESTED?
HOW ARE THE TESTS ORGANISED?
WHAT WILL THE TESTS INVOLVE?
WHAT HAPPENS TO THE RESULTS?

■ **WHY WILL MY CHILD BE TESTED?**

The National Curriculum has certainly brought testing back into fashion. It seems also to be bringing a return to traditional, written exams taken by pupils working against the clock. As they work their way through the new curriculum all children in state schools will be tested at the ages of seven, 11, 14 and 16. These tests will be the same throughout England and Wales. They are designed to check children's progress in the compulsory subjects of the new curriculum. At these ages, children will also be formally assessed by their own teachers against national guidelines. Their overall performance will be based on a combination of both the written tests and their teachers' assessments.

Of course, testing is not in itself new. In the past, many children used to take the 11+ examination in the last year of primary school. Examinations at 16 for national qualifications have long been the norm in schools. In addition, many schools devise and set their own tests to check on pupils' progress. So why the fuss about these new tests? One of the main reasons is that these are the first national tests for all children under 16 since the 11+ exam was abolished in most parts of the country. For most primary schools – which have been free from national tests of any sort for many years – they are a particularly big change.

It is also an important change because tests have a very direct effect on what is taught at school. Schools will inevitably direct teaching towards the knowledge and skills which are being tested. In other words, the curriculum and testing go together. That is not to say that teachers will only 'teach to the tests' without covering anything else, but they will always have one eye on what lies ahead.

So the new national tests are actually part of the National Curriculum, not just some sort of add-on. The reasons for introducing testing are the same as for the National Curriculum. The government wants to ensure that all children follow a broad range of subjects and are taught the key content within each of those subjects. National tests are a way of guaranteeing that schools are doing just that.

There is now fairly wide agreement between the political parties on the need for testing, although differences remain over its methods and purpose. According to the Conservative government which introduced testing, the three main purposes are:

★ to inform parents how their child is progressing.
★ to show teachers how each child in their class is getting on.
★ to give the public information on which to judge the effectiveness of schools.

It is the last of these which has caused most concern. Critics allege that the real reason for this kind of national testing is to allow the creation of league tables comparing the performance of schools. They argue that if testing was just about assessing children then it could be done more effectively by teachers using their own methods. This – they say – has always been done and is less disruptive to teaching and less traumatic for pupils.

Many teachers also argue that their own assessment is a better guide to children's achievements than a formal test, since many children do badly under such conditions. However, education ministers point out that in the first formal tests for seven-year-olds around one child in three gained a higher level in the tests than had been predicted by the teacher's assessment. However, this may be partly explained by the fact that children had progressed between the teacher's assessment at the start of the spring term and the tests at the start of the summer term. At this age, an extra term of schooling can account for quite a difference.

What about independent schools?
The new national tests are only compulsory in state schools, including all grant-maintained schools. Independent schools do not have to

do the tests, just as they do not have to follow the National Curriculum. However it looks as if many independent schools will decide to implement the tests, although they do not fit well with the common pattern of pupils, particularly boys, changing school at 13 rather than 11. At 16, the National Curriculum test will be the GCSE, so independent schools cannot ignore it.

■ HOW ARE THE TESTS ORGANISED?

Children can be tested in various ways and the National Curriculum uses several different types of test. Firstly there are relatively informal assesments made by your child's own teacher. Your child will probably be unaware that they are being assessed. Oral, written and practical work will all be taken into account. These 'teacher assessments', as they are known, will be made in accordance with the specific targets for each subject laid down in the National Curriculum.

The second type of testing is the timed, written test. These involve test papers which are set nationally and sent out to all schools. They are taken under 'controlled conditions'. This means that pupils are not allowed to confer or seek help from other sources and must give their answers within a set time. They will be marked by pupils' own teachers. These tests look set to become the norm for the National Curriculum.

A third type of test involves pupils undertaking practical tasks – either on their own or in small groups – while teachers monitor their performance. These task-based tests were the first to be introduced in the National Curriculum when testing began. That is why the new national tests are called Standard Assessment Tasks or SATs for short. But after schools found them time-consuming and problematic to carry out, there was a marked shift towards the more traditional, or so-called 'pencil-and-paper', tests. Although some task-based tests may continue for children at seven, it looks as if they will be dropped for older pupils.

Finally, pupils can be assessed on work done during the entire school year either at home or in the classroom. This is known as 'coursework' and it is a hallmark of the GCSE. Often pupils are able to do some of their coursework at home. This has brought complaints that some pupils are unfairly helped by parents. However, much coursework is also done at school, often under close supervision and against time-limits. Some GCSEs – particularly English – used to involve coursework contributing 100 per cent of the marks at GCSE. However the government has decided to limit the amount of coursework that can be counted towards the GCSE when it becomes part of National Curriculum testing in 1994. From that date, coursework will be limited to around 20 or 30 per cent of the final marks in most subjects.

Overall, there has been a significant shift towards the more traditional, pencil-and-paper tests. Testing at seven will continue to use other methods, but the pattern at 11, 14 and 16 looks set to be mainly timed, written tests.

When will my child be tested?

Once the new national tests are fully introduced, all children will be tested when the majority of pupils in their class are seven, 11, 14 and 16. This has been designed to fit the main points of change in most children's school life. So the first tests come at the end of the infant school. The second tests coincide with the transition from primary to secondary schools (although they fit less neatly in areas where the middle-school system operates and children transfer at 12 or 13). The third set of tests come after three years at secondary school and just before pupils embark on their GCSE courses. The final tests – marking the end of compulsory schooling – will be in most cases the GCSE.

These distinct phases in school life have been designated as 'key stages' in the new jargon which unfortunately accompanies the National Curriculum. You do not really need to know this jargon, although you may sometimes hear teachers using it. It will, though, be useful to get used to the new descriptions for each school year. Out go familiar phrases such as 'first year infants' or 'top juniors' and in come the rather less descriptive 'Year One, Year Two . . .' and so on. It works like this:

KEY STAGES IN THE NATIONAL CURRICULUM

KEY STAGE	Age of most pupils at end of school year		Class Description
ONE	from 6 to 7	(infants)	Years 1 and 2
TWO	from 8 to 11	(junior)	Years 3 to 6
THREE	from 12 to 14	(secondary)	Years 7 to 9
FOUR	from 15 to 16	(secondary)	Years 10 and 11

Clearly schools will usually test all children in the same year-group at the same time. So, strictly speaking, the new national tests take place not when your child is seven, 11 or 14, but when the majority of children in their class are that age. Your child may still be only six, 10 or 13. Equally they could be almost eight, 12 or 15.

This means younger children in the class – that is those with birthdays in the late spring or summer – will be at something of a disadvantage. You should bear this in mind when you receive the results of your child's tests. But try not to worry about this disadvantage. A few months may make a lot of difference in the early stages of school, but they become much less significant later on. Also – while you will obviously be interested in how your child is doing compared with others – what may be more important is the progress they are making relative to their own earlier achievements. Remember too that these tests are not designed – as the old 11+ was – to determine which sort of school your child should go to. Nor is it intended that they should be used to make children repeat a year as happens in some other countries.

How will my child be graded?
Your child's achievement in the new national tests will be recorded against a ten-point scale, in which Level One is the bottom rung and Level Ten is the top. The approximate aim is that the average child will be at Level Two by the age of seven and will move up one level roughly every two years. Only the most able pupils will reach Level Ten, although the majority should reach Level Six or Seven by the age of 16.

NATIONAL CURRICULUM LEVELS FOR THE AVERAGE PUPIL	
Age at end of year	Level
6	One
7*	Two
9	Three
11*	Four
13	Five
14*	Five/Six
15	Six
16*	Six/Seven
* = age at which pupils take national tests	

At present, pupils who take GCSEs are graded from 'A' at the top to 'G' at the bottom. Anything below that gets a 'U' for ungraded. For those who still think in O Level terms, grades 'A' to 'C' at GCSE are considered equivalent to an O Level pass. However, from 1994 GCSE grades will be converted to the National Curriculum ten-point scale. So a grade 'A' will become a Level Nine or Ten, a grade 'B' becomes Level Eight and so on. The lowest levels – from One to Three – will not earn a GCSE mark.

GCSE AND THE NATIONAL CURRICULUM
Until 1993 grades A (top) to G (lowest)
From 1994 levels 10 (top) to 4 (lowest)

GCSE		National Curriculum Level
A	=	9/10
B	=	8
C		7
D	=	
E		6
F	=	5
G	=	4
U	=	1, 2 and 3*

* these levels will not be assessed by the GCSE and will not appear on certificates.

It is clear from this that Level Ten is more difficult to reach than grade 'A'. So a new top grade – in effect an 'A+' – is being introduced to stretch and reward brighter pupils. Pupils will only get a GCSE certificate if they reach Level Four or above. Alternative tests are likely to be devised for pupils who are not considered able to reach this level. This is because it has been decided not to devise GCSEs which attempt to test achievement as far down as that expected of the average nine-year-old.

■ **WHAT WILL THE TESTS INVOLVE?**
The following applies to schools in England. In Wales, there will also be tests in Welsh. For children in Welsh-speaking schools, Welsh will be a core subject. In other schools it is a foundation subject.

At seven

The tests for seven-year olds were the first to be introduced, with all children of this age taking them in English, mathematics and science in 1991. This was a national trial and considerable changes have been made to the tests after protests from schools that they were taking too long to carry out. Originally there were more task-based tests done by children working in groups of four or five. These included a science task in which pupils had to predict if certain objects would sink or float and then test their predictions. Most of this type of test has now been dropped in favour of something more formal. Now there are more pencil-and-paper tests, many of which can be taken by much larger groups of children at once.

Seven-year-olds will be required to do the Standard Assessment Tasks only in the three core subjects of English, mathematics and science. In the other subjects they will be assessed by their own teachers using either their own methods, optional SATs or simply based on their work over the past year. As ever, teachers will be constantly assessing pupils on their normal class work. What is new, though is that this will now be done against National Curriculum guidelines, with pupils graded on the new ten-level scale. When the teacher's assessment is different from the score in the SAT, it is usually the latter that will count.

TESTS FOR SEVEN-YEAR-OLDS
The Standard Assessment Tasks will cover:
- Reading
- Writing
- Spelling
- Handwriting
- Mathematics
- Science

You will be given your child's score in all the nine National Curriculum subjects taught at primary school. The majority of pupils at this age are expected to reach Level Two, the level for the average seven-year-old. However more able children can be tested up to Level Three or Four and, very occasionally, even higher.

Schools can choose for themselves the precise time they do the tests, although it must be within the two half-terms either side of Easter, or roughly between early March and late May. The tests are designed so one teacher can complete them for an entire class within 30 hours. The tests will cover:

Reading
Children will take a test pitched at one of the first four levels of the National Curriculum. Those who are thought to be at around Level One will begin with a test based on a book they are already familiar with. To achieve Level One they will be expected to talk about the book, respond to questions, and pick out some words and some letters.

For Level Two, they will be asked to read aloud a passage of about 100 words to their teacher. The passage will be taken from one of a list of approved books (see page 196), but not from one the child already knows well. Pupils must read the passage with some fluency and with the teacher having to tell them no more than eight words. To give more detail on your child's reading, those who have reached Level Two – which is expected to be the majority – will be further graded from A to E for their accuracy on 25 key words in the passage. To get a grade A, children must get all 25 of the key words correct. It is expected that Level Two readers will divide fairly equally between these five divisions.

READING TESTS
- Read three signs (one of which must be a complete sentence) from around the classroom.
- Read aloud a 100-word passage from a graded book chosen by the teacher.
- Those reaching Level Two are marked for accuracy on 25 key words in the passage. The number of correct words required for each grade varies from book to book, but is roughly:
  A = all 25 right
  B = 23/24
  C = 21/22
  D = 18/20
  E = up to 18
- comprehension test optional at Level Two, but compulsory at Levels Three and Four.

For Levels Three and Four, children will be tested on books taken from two other lists (see page 197). To reach Level Three, pupils must be able to read the opening 50 words of the story fluently with no more than two hesitations or stumbles allowed. To reach Level Four the child should be able to read the 100-word passage clearly, fluently and accurately with varied expression and pace.

A written test of reading comprehension will also be available for children who are at Level Two, although its use is not compulsory. The comprehension test is compulsory at Levels Three and Four.

Writing and handwriting

Children will be asked to write a story on a topic suggested by the teacher. They will be told to write it for a particular audience, such as other children in the class. Work will be assessed for its content, clarity and standard of spelling and handwriting. Children who do very well in this test can be given the chance to redraft their stories. If they show a good understanding of how and why it can be improved, they gain Level Three.

WRITING TESTS
- children will be asked to write a story for a specific audience.
- those who do well at Level Two will be tested to see if they can improve their story with redrafting. If they do improve its clarity, they will reach Level Three.
- the story will also be used for assessing handwriting.

Spelling

A spelling test is being developed for children at Levels Three and Four. It can also be used for children at Level Two. The sort of words children should be able to spell include:

★ Level Two: see, car, man, hot, sun, cold, thank.

★ Level Three: because, after, open, teacher, animal, together.

★ Level Four: explain, extend, retake, recall, growing, doing.

Mathematics

The teacher will read out a list of additions, subtractions and multi-plications and the children will have five seconds to write down each answer. They will also have to complete worksheets which give number problems based on a visit to the greengrocers. For example, working out the change from 15p when buying two apples which cost 6p each.

At Level Three, they will be expected to add and subtract numbers up to 20 and to do multiplication up to $5 \times 5 = 25$.

MATHEMATICS TESTS
- mental arithmetic tests with the teacher reading out sums and pupils given five seconds to write down each answer e.g. $4 + 2$, $8 - 6$, 3×4.
- worksheets based on shopping at the greengrocer's shop. Children can use pencil and paper and calculators for some of these sums.
  and either
- a task involving sorting 20 or more objects (e.g. pencils, paper clips, a ruler etc) into different sets and counting and recording the numbers in each set.
  or
- a task involving spinners with numbers in which children have to work out the probability of landing on specific numbers.

Science

This will cover children's knowledge of different materials and the Earth and atmosphere. So, for example, an average seven-year-old might be expected to group materials according to their physical characteristics, such as those that decay naturally and those that do not. They might also be asked to show their understanding of the weather and the way it affects natural materials and people's lives.

SCIENCE TESTS
Either
- a task involving describing, grouping and comparing a range of objects (e.g. spoons, pebbles, rubber bands, string etc.) according to colour, texture, shape, and weight and what happens to them when heated/cooled.
- for those at Level Three, categorising objects according to whether they are manufactured or natural.
  or
- the teacher asks children to talk or write about the weather and its effects on our lives.
- tasks involving recording observations about the weather.

The 1991 results

Although the tests have changed since then, the results of the 1991 SATs give the clearest picture so far of the levels achieved by seven-year-olds. Averaging out the results in English, mathematics and science, 79 per cent of children in England were at or above Level Two. In other words, more than three-quarters of pupils had reached – or bettered – the level expected of the typical seven-year-old. This was, of course, a trial run for the tests and experts accept they may not have pitched all the levels correctly. In science it seems the tests may have been too easy.

1991 TEST RESULTS
Level 1 = average for 5-year-old
Level 2 = average for 7-year-old
Level 3 = average for 9-year-old
English
Level 1   21 per cent
Level 2   61 per cent
Level 3   17 per cent
Mathematics
Level 1   25 per cent
Level 2   66 per cent
Level 3   6 per cent
Science
Level 1   9 per cent
Level 2   67 per cent
Level 3   22 per cent

(Figures do not add up to 100 per cent because figures are rounded up or down and a small number of pupils did not reach level 1).

Within the overall picture, there are some interesting variations. In reading, 28 per cent of children failed to reach the level expected of seven-year-olds. This was a higher proportion than for other aspects of English. Overall, girls did better than boys in all subjects. In reading the gap was particularly wide with 78 per cent of girls achieving Level Two or better compared to 66 per cent of boys. The other big variation was from one part of the country to another. The top local education authority was Richmond-upon-Thames where 88 per cent of pupils reached Level Two or above. This contrasted with Bradford at the bottom with just 59 per cent. The extent to which this reflects more effective teaching rather than other factors such as social conditions, school-starting age and the availability of nursery education is impossible to tell on the basis of the raw figures alone.

At eleven

The first national standard tests for 11-year-olds will not happen until 1994. So far little detail is available as the government is waiting to see how testing at seven and 14 goes first. However, it is expected that – as at seven – SATs will only be compulsory in English, mathematics and science. It is also expected that the tests will be mainly written, pencil-and-paper style tests. Pupils' progress in these and all other subjects will also be assessed by their own teachers on the basis of normal class work over the years, although some optional SATs may well be available for teachers who wish to use them. These teacher assessments will be made according to the new National Curriculum guidelines and will be based on the new ten-level scale.

At fourteen

The first full round of tests for 14-year-olds takes place in 1993, although a trial run in mathematics and science was due in June 1992. From 1993 there will be tests in mathematics, science, English, and technology. Formal tests in history and geography are due to start in 1994 and in modern foreign languages in 1995. There will probably not be formal tests in music, art or physical education.

The tests will be traditional, written papers taken by all 14-year-olds under examination conditions on set days. Multiple choice questions may be used in the science tests. Most tests will last about one hour each and they will be marked by pupils' own teachers. Grades will be from one to ten on the National Curriculum scale. There will be four different versions of each test, each appropriate for pupils of different ability. These will cover levels 1–4, 3–6, 5–8 and 7–10. Schools will choose which papers pupil sit, according to assessments already made by teachers. The aim is that pupils should not have to answer questions which are significantly below their ability. Because the tests are in traditional form, some aspects of the new curriculum – speaking and listening skills in English, for example – will not be formally tested. The same will be true of problem-solving skills in mathematics and science.

As well as taking the written tests, pupils will be assessed by their own teachers throughout the first three years of secondary school. This of course is not new. What is new is that the assessments will be made against the new national guidelines and according to the new ten-level scale. A pupil's final mark at 14 will be based on an aggregate of the formal test result and the teacher's assessment.

TESTS FOR 14-YEAR-OLDS
From 1993
- mathematics: three tests of one hour each.
- science: three tests of one hour each.
- English: a one-hour reading comprehension test.
- English: two 90-minute tests of writing ability, including spelling and handwriting/presentation.
- technology: one test of 90 minutes and one of one hour.
- Welsh (Wales only): three 45-minute tests plus oral and written tasks spread over a longer period.

Later
- history, geography and a modern foreign language.

At sixteen – The GCSE

The fourth and final round of tests in the National Curriculum are taken by most pupils when they are 16. For most pupils the tests will be the existing GCSEs, although these are being adapted to make sure they cover all aspects of the new curriculum. Other examinations broadly equivalent to GCSEs may also be used, particularly where pupils are taking short courses or are combining subjects into a joint course.

The first new-style GCSEs – covering English language, mathematics, and science – will be taken in 1994. So the new, two-year GCSE syllabuses will begin in September 1992.

In future, many more pupils will take GCSEs as it becomes compulsory for the large majority of pupils to sit tests at 16 in English, mathematics and science. The exception will be those pupils who are not expected to reach Level Four, the equivalent of a grade G at GCSE. For them, the GCSE will be too difficult and some other form of test will probably be found. With all pupils also required to study a foreign language and technology to 16, many more will also take GCSEs in these subjects, though this is not compulsory.

Another important change is being made to the GCSE as it becomes the National Curriculum test for 16-year-olds. In order to pitch questions at the appropriate level for pupils of different abilities, there will be different examination papers. Teachers will decide which is the appropriate paper for each pupil to take. They will use results from the tests at 14 to help them decide this. So, for example, a brighter pupil might be put in for a GCSE which is pitched at Levels Six to Ten. A less able pupil may be entered for a GCSE which, for example, will test pupils between Levels Three and Eight. There are likely to be three or four different ranges of GCSE, although the precise number has not yet been decided.

Some say this change amounts to a return to the old division between O Levels and the CSE. It will certainly ensure that pupils are not faced with questions that are either too easy or too difficult for them. However, there is potential for disagreement between parents and teachers over the level of exam pupils should be entered for, particularly as a pupil taking a GCSE covering Levels Three to Eight would probably not be able to score a Level Nine or Ten.

Will Coursework Still Count?

One distinctive aspect of the GCSE is that work done by the pupils during the year – either at school or at home – counts towards their final examination mark. This has proved popular with many teachers and pupils, as it allows a wider spread of work to be assessed. In English, for example, pupils can read much more widely and can choose to write about the authors they are most interested in. There is less time spent on revising two or three set texts, as used to be the case at O level. Coursework also allows pupils to draft and re-draft their work, a skill that is specifically encouraged by the National Curriculum and is useful in many occupations.

In practical, problem-solving subjects like technology, the use of coursework is particularly helpful. According to Peter Chester, head of technology at Colchester Royal Grammar School, coursework's greatest value is 'in the motivation it gives to pupils who are able to choose the projects they want to work on and then develop the skills needed'. His GCSE pupils have been involved in designing and making items such as a remote-controlled robotic arm, a hovercraft and an automatic cat-feeder. Half of their GCSE marks are given for these practical projects.

Traditionalists have argued that coursework allows pupils to be helped by parents or to rely too heavily on regurgitating material from reference books. This was not always a fair criticism as some coursework was done under controlled conditions at school.

All GCSEs must give a minimum of 20 per cent of marks for coursework done either at home or at school and marked by pupil's own teachers. In the past 100 per cent coursework was possible. In English, for example, half of all pupils were doing coursework-only CGSEs. But the government believed that there was no guarantee of even standards across the country with coursework which is set and marked by individual teachers in individual schools (although it is checked by outside examiners). So, for pupils taking their GCSEs in 1994 and after, there will be a maximum of between 20 and 60 per cent for coursework in most subjects.

The exact amount varies from subject to subject. In English language the coursework ceiling is 40 per cent and in English literature it is 30 per cent. In more practical subjects, rather more coursework is allowed. In technology, for example, there will be a minimum of 40 per cent and a maximum of 60 per cent.

Will Poor Spelling Lose Marks?
There has been growing concern recently over standards of spelling, punctuation and grammar amongst school-leavers. Recent practice has been to deduct marks for poor performance in these areas only in English. It is argued that it is unfair to handicap pupils in other subjects. But the government has now required GCSE boards to deduct marks for consistently poor grammar, punctuation and spelling. Five per cent or more marks could be lost, although the exact amount has not yet been decided and may vary from subject to subject. From 1993 pupils will not be allowed to take spell-checkers or dictionaries into examinations.

Are GCSE Standards Lower than O Level?
Each year, as the proportion of pupils getting good grades at GCSE rises, there is a renewed chorus of complaint that the standards it sets are too low. In particular, there are those who call for a return to the old O Level which they say had more academic rigour. Others – including most teachers – say pass-rates are improving because most pupils respond well to the GCSE and deny charges of falling standards.

It is impossible to arbitrate in this fierce argument. The simple fact is that they are very different kinds of examination. The O Level put more emphasis on the recall of factual knowledge. The GCSE – with its strong coursework element – sets greater store on the development of skills. It allows children to show what they can do – and rewards them for that – rather than testing to see if they can recall, understand and use a particular set of facts.

The other difference is that the O level was specifically designed for the brighter and more academic children. Others took the CSE. The GCSE, by contrast, is designed for pupils of all abilities. So it is undoubtedly true that some GCSE questions are easier than O level questions, but different questions are aimed at different pupils. Some people argue that it is not sensible to aim one examination at all pupils. The National Curriculum goes some way to accepting this, since pupils will be assessed by their teachers and then given test papers at a level appropriate to their ability.

Much of the argument over standards has been caused by the initial equation of a GCSE grade C or above with an O Level pass. However because of the different nature of these two examinations, this sort of parallel is of limited value. The fact is that GCSE grades are improving and this has coincided with a welcome increase in the proportion of youngsters staying on in full-time education, now at about 60 per cent.

GCSE PASS RATES IN 1991

GCSE Grade	percentage of pupils who took examination
Grade A	11.6 per cent
Grade A–C	49.0 per cent
Grade A–G	97.8 per cent

(O Level pass rate in 1987: 39.8 per cent)

Overall, more than one in three 16-year-olds manage five or more GCSEs at grade C or better. At the bottom end, only around one pupil in 14 fails to get even one grade G. Pass-rates do vary from one part of the country to another. The Department of Education recently published a league table of education authorities based on the proportion of pupils getting five or more GCSEs at grade C or better. The top authority managed almost 40 per cent, while the bottom one gained less than nine per cent.

■ WHAT HAPPENS TO THE RESULTS?

As a parent, you have the right to see your child's National Curriculum test results at seven, 11 and 14. Schools are now required to give you an annual, written report on your child from the age of 5 to 14. This must cover your child's progress in all National Curriculum subjects and give test results. GCSE results will be sent to your home by the examination boards. When your child leaves school they will also be given a Record of Achievement which they can show to prospective employers. This will detail all test and examination results and record achievements in all National Curriculum and other subjects, as well as your child's interest and involvement in other activities and hobbies.

As well as giving results to parents, schools must also publish the overall results of tests at 11, 14 and at GCSE. This has to be done in a standard way so that parents can compare the record of different schools. However, schools do not have to publish overall results for seven-year-olds, although the government has urged them to do so.

League tables of schools' examinations record are now being produced by national and local newspapers. This has been encouraged by Conservative politicians who propose to require education authorities to publish performance league tables of all schools in their locality, including independent schools and City Technology Colleges. This will include tables of National Curriculum test results, GCSE and A level examinations and truancy levels. It will also show how many school-leavers enter employment. Full details of these tables must be kept in local libraries and summary tables will appear in newspapers.

Many educationalists are unhappy about the proposed league tables. They argue that these will only tell parents how academically selective a school is, not how well it is educating pupils. Clearly there is some force in this. A grammar school which takes only the top 15 per cent of pupils will be very high on any league table whatever the quality of its teaching. Equally a comprehensive in a socially deprived area may well have excellent teaching but its results may leave it low in any league table.

Some people say it would be best if league tables took account of the social or academic background of pupils and weighted results accordingly. Others say it would be best to give a 'value-added' version, showing the level of school-leavers test results in relation to their ability levels on arrival at the school. Conservative ministers say all this is unnecessary as parents can rely on their common sense when judging between the results of, say, Eton College and an inner-city comprehensive. Whatever happens, though, it is clear that unofficial league tables at least are here to stay as the public's appetite has been whetted and editors clearly believe they help sell newspapers!

6
ENGLISH

■

WHAT DOES ENGLISH INVOLVE?

WHAT WILL MY CHILD STUDY?

WHAT WILL MY CHILD BE EXPECTED TO KNOW?

■ **WHAT DOES ENGLISH INVOLVE?**

English is the most important subject your child will be taught at school. Reading, writing and the ability to listen carefully and speak with clarity are all skills that are essential not only for learning about all other subjects, but also for a successful and fulfilling life. That is why English – alongside mathematics and science – is one of the so-called 'core' subjects in the National Curriculum. This means it will be compulsory for all children from five to 16. What is more, virtually all youngsters must follow a GCSE course in English.

The aspects of English that all children must be taught fall into three areas:

Speaking and listening
Reading
Writing (including spelling and handwriting)

Speaking and listening

The idea of placing speaking and listening alongside the more traditional reading and writing may surprise many parents. In recent years, increasing emphasis has been put on spoken communication and the part it plays in children's development, both educationally and socially. But why does it matter? For a start, there are ties between the development of spoken language and learning to read. Also most people accept that the ability to express oneself and give or receive information is important in most jobs. Certainly employers have made it clear they value it. In everyday life away from work we also need to be able to express ourselves and understand others, whether it be at the bank, the shop or the travel agent. At a more sophisticated level, it is useful to understand how people can use language for emotive effect or to persuade you to do something. Think, for example, of a politician or a time-share salesman.

Reading
Nothing is more important than reading. One of the main aims will be to teach and encourage children to read on their own. As described in the chapter on primary schools, there is a fierce debate over the best way to teach children to read. The National Curriculum does not explicitly favour or exclude any one approach. In fact, it urges teachers to use a whole range of 'cues' or aids to recognising words. Despite this, a few critics believe it fails to put as much emphasis as they would like on the sounding-out of individual letters, such as 'kuh-ah-tuh' equals 'cat'.

Most primary school teachers believe the new curriculum endorses current practice which favours teaching children to read through several different approaches. Certainly, the National Curriculum says children should learn to recognise words through the sounds of letters (phonic cues), the shapes of whole words (the look-and-say approach), the use of picture aids, and from the wider context or meaning of the passage they are reading.

In the primary school, your child should be surrounded by examples of the written word, either on labels, signs, or in books. Plenty of easily accessible and well displayed books are a sign of a good infants' classroom. Children should be encouraged to read in order to obtain information and for enjoyment. Your child's teacher – and sometimes other adults in the classroom – should hear your child read individually on a regular basis. My own daughter's teacher has the excellent practice of encouraging parents to stay on for the first 15 minutes of the day to hear their own child read. This is a good way of settling the class down at the start of the day and gets parents who cannot give up a whole morning to help a chance to feel more involved and comfortable in the classroom.

Most schools also arrange for children to take books home for you to read with them. This is one of the main areas where you can really help your child to progress. If you show a lack of interest – or somehow do not often manage to find time – do not be surprised if your child loses interest too. At the secondary level, schools are supposed to encourage reading outside the classroom, either at home or in libraries. Pupils will increasingly be encouraged to think

WHAT PARENTS CAN DO TO HELP WITH READING

- switch off the television and do some reading yourself (and not just the newspaper!) – you are an important role model.
- give and read books to your baby – they can enjoy them without understanding them and board or cloth books are almost indestructible!
- take your child to the public library regularly.
- buy books for your children and encourage others to give books rather than sweets as presents.
- make reading together an enjoyable experience: don't correct every mistake or insist that children read even when they are tired.
- short, regular reading sessions are better than one big splurge when guilt catches up with you!
- discuss the contents of the book to encourage comprehension – but do not make it a formal test.
- look carefully at books before choosing them, looking for interesting stories and well laid-out pages.
- once they can read, buy a children's dictionary and an encyclopedia (not at this stage a huge, multi-volume set which may be overwhelming) and encourage your child to use them.
- some recommended authors for primary school children include: Janet and Allan Ahlberg, Jane Hissey, Shirley Hughes, Arnold Lobel, Jill Murphy, and Maurice Sendak. But there are many, many other marvellous writers too. Ask your local children's librarian if you need advice.

critically about the texts they read, analysing style and form. The reading of poetry is explicitly encouraged by the National Curriculum.

For helpful reading lists for children of various ages you can write (with a stamped self-addressed envelope) to The Reading and Language Information Centre, University of Reading, London Road, Reading RG1 5AQ. The former director of this centre, Betty Root, is an acknowledged expert on reading. Her excellent book *Help Your Child Learn to Read* (Usborne) gives sensible and helpful advice.

Writing
This area of English covers both the creative process of writing and the 'building-bricks' of writing, including spelling and handwriting.

The two go together. Teachers will be looking to develop both good creative writing and improved spelling, grammar and handwriting as pupils progress. The aim is to ensure that children are increasingly able to write coherently about a wide range of topics and to adapt their writing to different purposes and audiences. As they progress, children will be taught how to plan, draft and revise a piece of writing. These skills will of course be very important when it comes to GCSEs and other examinations, either in timed essays or in coursework.

As far as *spelling* is concerned, the aim of the National Curriculum is that by 16 pupils should be able to spell most of the words they are likely to need in their writing. They should also be able to make a sensible attempt to spell words they have not seen before and to check for misspelling in a dictionary. Pupils will lose marks for poor spelling in GCSEs in other subjects as well as English. With *handwriting*, the aim is to achieve a fluent, legible style rather than to move towards the artistic qualities of calligraphy.

■ WHAT YOUR CHILD WILL STUDY
From five to seven
In the infants, your child will develop *speaking and listening* skills through a range of activities including classroom discussion, listening to radio programmes, role-playing, and speaking and listening to one another. As a parent you may hardly notice what is happening. But during the normal, everyday goings-on of the classroom children are learning to listen carefully and to follow instructions. Activities which might seem to you to be play – such as learning songs or poems – are helping to develop speaking and listening skills.

ACTIVITIES TO ENCOURAGE SPEAKING AND LISTENING
- listening and responding to stories, poems, rhymes and songs.
- responding to television and radio.
- discussion of their own work.
- reciting poems and stories learnt by heart.
- describing experiences such as a family outing.
- improvising drama.
- giving and receiving instructions.

The aim at this age is to teach your child to relate events or instructions in the proper order and to increase the clarity of their argument. They will also be encouraged to speak up and to speak out clearly. As with most aspects of the National Curriculum for this age group, there may not be separate lessons on individual subjects. So rather than having a time set aside for English, children will develop the skills of speaking and listening while doing all sorts of other activities, such as science, history or geography.

In *reading*, children of this age are expected to build on what they have learnt at home. Teachers are expected to use a variety of books, both fiction and non-fiction. They should make sure children regularly hear stories and poems told or read aloud to them. As well as books, children should be reading their own writing and signs, labels, or notices around the classroom. The National Curriculum encourages parents to share in their child's reading.

ACTIVITIES FOR READING FROM FIVE TO SEVEN
- listening to stories or poems read aloud.
- sharing reading with other pupils and the teacher.
- reading during role-playing activities (e.g. reading a menu in a restaurant).
- reading signs and labels.
- making their own books.
- using word-books or simple dictionaries.
- reading aloud and silently.

At this age, *writing* will come into all sorts of different activities in the classroom. Children will write their names on their own paintings and write labels for wall displays. They will write on their own and copy words written by their teacher. Most will start by forming individual letters in lower case rather than capitals. Some schools, though, are encouraging children to work towards joined-up writing from the very start. This usually begins by learning the shape of individual letters with the 'flicks' or beginnings of a join already attached. Then, as soon as they are ready, the children are encouraged to join up letters. Some believe teaching joined-up writing immediately will confuse children, but others point to its success in other European countries and say it makes it much easier later on when children do have to learn to write fluently.

Throughout the primary school children should be taught how

to draft and re-draft their writing. This involves them making judgments on their own work and then setting about improving it to make it clearer to others. The new curriculum also requires children of all ages to write on a word processor.

ACTIVITIES FOR WRITING FROM FIVE TO SEVEN
- writing diaries, stories, letters and accounts of their activities.
- writing lists, labels, posters and greetings cards.
- learning about grammatical terms such as: sentence, verb, tense, noun.
- discussing what they have written.

From seven to eleven

Once again, at this age English may often be woven in to activities and projects covering other subjects, like science or history. So – for example – speaking and listening skills can be developed as children listen to instructions for a science activitity and as they discuss and report their findings.

In *speaking and listening*, your child will be encouraged to learn how to express views with increasing sophistication, to assess and interpret arguments, to follow and give increasingly precise instructions and to present information in a clear and systematic way.

ACTIVITIES IN SPEAKING AND LISTENING FROM SEVEN TO 11
- expressing and justifying feelings and opinions.
- assessing and interpreting arguments with increasing discrimination.
- giving and receiving increasingly complex instructions.
- reciting and reading aloud with fluency.
- taking on roles in a drama.
- discussing issues and trying to reach agreement.

In *reading*, from the age of seven to 11 children should be encouraged to broaden the range of books they are using. They will be encouraged to develop their own preferences in the choice of books and to become more independent in their reading. By this stage, they might also be introduced to poetry which was not specifically written for children. By 11, the average pupil should know how to read a contents page or use an index.

ACTIVITIES FOR READING FROM SEVEN TO 11

- selecting their own books for reading.
- keeping records of their own reading and commenting on what they have read.
- reading aloud to the class.
- checking for their own mistakes.
- learning differnt kinds of reading (e.g. 'search' reading to find a particular fact in a non-fiction book).

In *writing*, from seven onwards more attention will be given to punctuation (capital letters, full stops, question marks) and spelling. Children will be encouraged to check their own spellings with dictionaries. Once they can print letters fluently, they should develop a joined-up style of handwriting.

ACTIVITIES FOR WRITING FROM SEVEN TO 11

- writing and laying out letters to known people.
- writing chronological accounts of personal experiences.
- checking spellings in a dictionary or with a computer spell-checker.
- writing, revising and laying out stories or items for, say, a class newspaper.

From 11 to 14

In speaking and listening, your child will continue with the same sort of activities as before. The difference is that the teacher will be trying to develop greater sophistication of expression and will expect pupils to be able to give – and respond to – more complex information. In particular, there will begin to be emphasis on the variety of accent and dialect in the English language. Spoken contributions to the class are expected to be more reasoned and questions more probing.

ACTIVITIES FOR SPEAKING AND LISTENING FROM 11 TO 14

- make longer contributions to class or group discussions.
- make formal presentations, e.g. role-play or scripted scenes.
- learn about specialised vocabulary belonging to particular occupations, groups or local communities.

In *reading*, from 11 onwards your child should be starting to manage a variety of different kinds of book, including autobiographies, letters, and diaries as well as stories and poems. They should also be introduced to books written in the last century or before. This should include reading classics, such as the Bible, Wordsworth's poems or the novels of Charles Dickens. They should also be introduced to some of Shakespeare's plays.

Pupils should be taught to recognise that different types of language are used in different media. They should also recognise that the English language is constantly changing over time and they should understand how words are being used and for what aims. With non-fiction, they should become increasingly adept at finding information.

ACTIVITIES FOR READING FROM 11 TO 14
- reading some of the classics of English literature.
- tackling difficult texts, including those aimed at adults and written pre-twentieth century.
- reading a range of materials, such as newspapers, magazines, dictionaries, brochures, atlases.
- learning to skim-read when searching for a fact.
- analysing the use of language and literary styles.

From 11 onwards, children should be developing the range and proficiency of their *writing*. They will be taught to plan, draft and revise when attempting longer pieces of writing. They should also become aware of the different purposes of writing, such as for communicating knowledge and information or for conveying imaginative ideas.

ACTIVITIES FOR WRITING FROM 11 TO 14
- writing in a wide variety of forms, e.g. notes, diaries, letters, book reviews, advertisements, poems, plays.
- developing elements in story structure, e.g. opening, setting, characters, events and an ending.
- writing and correcting on a word processor.
- learning to use more sophisticated punctuation, such as semi-colons and colons.

rom 14 to 16

In *speaking and listening*, youngsters should by now be learning far greater sophistication of expression. Classroom activities should give them the chance to deliver and comprehend more complex verbal accounts. They will learn to appreciate why inappropriate language can have an unintended effect. There will also be more emphasis on undertaking formal and responsible roles, for example addressing visitors to the school or making a formal presentation to large groups.

ACTIVITIES FOR SPEAKING AND LISTENING FROM 14 TO 16
- taking part in group discussion, including taking notes and checking back with the group that they represent the consensus.
- trying out and discussing when it is appropriate to use Standard English (in formal settings) and when non-standard varieties can be used (with friends, in dialogue in a play).
- taking part in debates with a formal structure.

Reading will now be broadening to include texts written for adults, including literary classics. They should be recognising different literary styles. They should also be acting as literary detectives, working out the author's point of view from the use of language in, for example, the leader columns of a newspaper or political pamphlets. They should also be taught how words develop and why vocabulary changes over the years.

ACTIVITIES FOR READING FROM 14 TO 16
- reading 'difficult' texts, such as Shakespeare.
- recognising literary devices (e.g. alliteration, metaphors, onomatopoeia).
- analysing newspaper leaders, promotional material etc.
- recognising authorial standpoints from the text.
- understanding dialect and changing fashions of written language.
- understanding ambiguity.

For their *writing*, pupils in the last years of the National Curriculum should be taught to recognise that writing is often more formal than speech and that grammatical structures are needed to emphasise key points in a written sentence. They should become adept at writing in different styles appropriate for their audience.

ACTIVITIES FOR WRITING FROM 14 TO 16
- writing in a wider range of forms, e.g. newspaper articles, poems, essays, autobiography etc.
- learning to craft their writing so it is pleasurable and easy to read.
- developing imaginative writing.

■ WHAT YOUR CHILD IS EXPECTED TO KNOW

Remember that children develop at varying speeds. In other words, progress will probably come in uneven bursts. Also remember that while you will want to know what is 'average' at a particular age, it is just as important to know whether or not your child is progressing relative to their own earlier achievements.

At seven

Children take the first national tests – the Standard Assessment Tasks, or SATs – at the end of the infant school, when most are seven. The tests will cover reading, writing, spelling and hand-writing. Speaking and listening will be assessed by the children's own teacher during normal class-time.

Many of the tests will be of the pencil-and-paper variety so that a large group of children, or even the whole class, can be tested at the same time. Standardised worksheets will be sent to schools. The tests are pitched at different levels. Children will initially be given tests according to the level their teachers predict they will achieve. But all children who score at the upper end of a level will then be given tests at the next level above. Children of this age can be tested up to *Level Four*.

In reading, children will be tested on books which are graded at Levels One to Four and are taken from an authorised list of titles (see page 196). At *Level One*, they are expected to be able to respond to questions about the contents of a book they are already familiar with and to pick out some individual words and letters. Children at this level are not yet considered able to read independently.

For *Level Two*, they will read aloud a 100-word passage from one of the authorised books. Teachers are not supposed to use a book the child is familiar with. (See page 68 for more details.) Since *Level Two* is a very broad category, children can also be graded from A to E on their ability to read 25 key words in the passage.

Children of above average ability will be tested to see if they have reached *Level Three* (the average for a nine-year-old) or *Level Four* (the average for an 11-year-old). A separate spelling test is compulsory for children reaching *Level Three* and *Four*. Teachers may if they wish use this test for children at *Level Two* also. Overall, the average seven-year-old should be at *Level Two*. To achieve that they should, amongst other things, be able to do the following:

Speaking and Listening
★ speak/listen in a group activity, such as making up a story together.
★ describe an event that happened at home or on television.
★ say what they like or dislike about a story they have heard.
★ understand more complex instructions (e.g. 'Write down the place in the classroom where you think your plant will grow best, find out what the others think and try to agree on which is likely to be the best place').

Reading
★ show knowledge of the alphabet (e.g. in using a dictionary, knowing the order of letters).
★ read a range of material without help and with some fluency, accuracy and understanding.
★ describe what has happened in a story and predict what might happen next.

Writing
★ write complete sentences, some with capital letters and full stops.
★ write a simple story with a clear beginning, characters and one or more events.
★ spell correctly simple words e.g. car, man, sun, hot, cold, thank.
★ write legible and consistent letters, in both lower case and capitals.

At eleven
Towards the end of primary school, when most pupils in the class are 11, children will take their second set of national, written tests. Since the tests for 11-year-olds do not start until 1994, few details are known. As well as these formal tests, children will be assessed by their own teacher during normal class work. These assessments will cover all aspects of English, including speaking and listening, which cannot be tested by written examination.

The average 11-year-old should have reached *Level Four* in the

National Curriculum. To achieve that, they should – amongst other things – be able to:

Speaking and Listening
★ give an oral report on, say, a class activity to another group of pupils.
★ ask and answer questions in more demanding situations, such as on a mock radio programme.
★ improvise a scene from a story.

Reading
★ read aloud expressively and fluently from a range of familiar books.
★ describe the qualities of a story or poem that they particularly like.
★ find books in the library by using the classification system.
★ find factual information by means of search reading.

Writing
★ show proper use of simple structure and punctuation e.g. titles, paragraphs, full stops, question marks, and quotation marks for direct speech.
★ use more formal sentence structures, such as subordinate clauses.
★ organise words on the page for different purposes e.g. letters, poems, invitations.
★ spell correctly longer words which follow common patterns e.g. because, after, teacher, animal.
★ recognise word families (e.g. grow, growth, growing, grown).
★ recognise regular patterns in spelling i.e. prefixes and suffixes, such as pre- and -ing.
★ produce legible joined-up writing.

At fourteen
At 14 pupils face their third national tests in English. The current plan is for them to take a one-hour written test to assess their reading, and two tests of 90 minutes each to test writing, including spelling and handwriting. Assessments will also be made of normal class work by teachers. These will cover all aspects of English, including speaking and listening.

An average 14-year-old should be somewhere between *Level Five* and *Level Six* on the National Curriculum ten-point scale. To achieve that they should, amongst other things, be able to:

Speaking and Listening
★ argue for or against a point of view.
★ convey information effectively (e.g. an eye-witness account of an incident).
★ contribute to a discussion while responding to and developing the views of others.

Reading
★ read a range of fiction and poetry explaining and justifying their preferences.
★ show an awareness of a writer's choice of particular words and the effect on the reader.
★ select reference books and follow up factual inquiries.
★ recognise the difference between fact and opinion.

Writing
★ produce independent work with correct use of layout, headings, paragraphs, and simple punctuation.
★ show an ability to assemble ideas on paper, then draft and revise them.
★ recognise differences in vocabulary (e.g. slang) and know when it is appropriate to use them.
★ spell correctly more complex, multi-syllabic words (e.g. medicine, muscular, historical, grammar).
★ produce clear, fluent handwriting and present work attractively.

At sixteen
At 16 – the age when pupils reach the end of the National Curriculum and take their English GCSE – the average pupil should be somewhere between *Level Six* and *Level Seven*. After 1994 the current GCSE grades of A to G will be replaced by the National Curriculum ten-point scale. Level Seven is equivalent to grades C/D and Level Six approximates to grades D/E. To reach Level Six/ Seven your child should, amongst other things, be able to:

Speaking and Listening
★ contribute constructively to group discussions.
★ adapt explanations for different audiences (e.g. an adult or a younger child).
★ adapt language to the situation (e.g. a job interview or an argument with a friend).

Reading
★ read a range of fiction, poetry and non-fiction, including pre-20th-century writing.
★ show they are developing insights e.g. making judgements about characters in a novel and being able to justify these by reference to the text.
★ recognise and understand the use of literary devices, such as metaphors, alliteration, rhyme.

Writing
★ write in appropriate way for different audiences e.g. for a younger child.
★ write with a clear sense of purpose, for example to 'compare and contrast'.
★ display well-developed choice of vocabulary.
★ spell and understand common roots borrowed from other languages e.g. micro-, psych-, therm-.

The most able pupils capable of getting an A grade at GCSE must reach *Level Nine or Ten* on the National Curriculum scale. Effectively a pupil at Level Ten has scored an A+ grade. To reach Level Nine/Ten your child should, amongst other things, be able to:

Speaking and Listening
★ give a clear and cogent presentation on a complex subject using notes and visual aids.
★ take an active part in a group discussion, recognising and helping to develop the views of others.
★ take a variety of roles, including chairing a group discussion.

Reading
★ show an understanding of literary devices and structures used by authors in a range of poetry, fiction and drama.
★ compare the treatment by different authors of similar themes.
★ show an understanding of styles in non-literary contexts, such as television news broadcasts.

Writing
★ write in a variety of forms, showing an ability to sustain the interest of the reader.
★ organise and present complex subject matter.
★ use a variety of sentence construction and an extensive vocabulary.

7
MATHEMATICS
■

WHAT DOES MATHEMATICS INVOLVE?

WHAT WILL MY CHILD STUDY?

WHAT WILL MY CHILD BE EXPECTED TO KNOW?

■ WHAT DOES MATHEMATICS INVOLVE?

Mathematics is one of the three core subjects in the National Curriculum. This means it is compulsory from the age of five right through to 16, ending for most pupils with the GCSE examination.

In many ways, mathematics is one of the most traditional school subjects. Addition, subtraction, multiplication and division are all still included, with a new emphasis on mental arithmetic or 'working in the head'. But mathematics is more than just arithmetic. It is aso a way of equipping youngsters with the means to tackle a range of practical problems. It can be used not only to explain why things happen but also to predict what will happen.

The new curriculum encourages mathematical skills to be taught in real-life situations. So, for example, pupils can learn through handling money when shopping or when weighing or measuring materials. There is also strong emphasis on problem-solving. But it is not all about the practical application of mathematics. Pupils will be taught to appreciate the structure of mathematics itself, for example by exploring number patterns. So, besides its practical uses, mathematics also encourages mental agility.

The central place of mathematics in the National Curriculum reflects the importance of mathematical skills to other subjects. Measurement and symmetry, for example, are important in design and technology. Statistical methods are important in science, geography and history.

The use of calculators is encouraged right from the start of primary school. Indeed they are now regular items of classroom equip-

93

ment and pupils will need to use them throughout the National Curriculum. While some say reliance on calculators has brought a decline in mental arithmetic skills, it is widely accepted that they enable more ambitious exploration of numbers and save time in making calculations. However, pupils will be taught to use mental arithmetic to estimate for expected answers in order to ensure they are of roughly the right order and that decimal points are in the right place. So both mental arithmetic and calculators are well established in the new curriculum.

The majority of primary schools spend about one-fifth of teaching time on mathematics. It is taught separately more often than any other subject. However it is sometimes also taught through topic or project work, involving English and science as well. A primary school topic might, for example, involve children taking to school items that involve numbers, such as receipts, bus tickets, pools forms and so on. They might then be asked to observe and discuss the meanings of the various numbers and to go on to explore measures, prices and sizes. Primary school children will also make use of classroom computers for mathematical work.

In secondary schools, mathematics will probably take up just over ten per cent of the timetable, although no minimum time is specified. Nor does the National Curriculum require pupils to be 'streamed' or grouped by ability for mathematics. Early signs from schools suggest no clear pattern of response to the new curriculum, with some schools switching from mixed ability teaching (where children of a range of abilities are taught together) to 'streaming' and others moving in the opposite direction.

The new curriculum divides mathematics into these five main areas:

Using and applying mathematics
This encourages the practical use of mathematics in everyday tasks. Your child will be taught how to use and develop mathematical reasoning and logic. Most teachers believe that applying mathematics to real situations improves learning.

Number
As well as counting, addition, subtraction, multiplication, and division, this also covers measurement, estimation and approximation. Pupils are expected to be able to do calculations in their heads, using pencil-and-paper and electronic calculators.

Algebra
This covers mathematical patterns and relationships, involving the use of symbolic representations. Your child will be introduced to formulae and equations and terms such as 'square', 'square root', 'multiple' and 'factor'.

Shape and space
Your child will learn about the properties of two- and three-dimensional shapes. They will learn about triangles, hexagons, cuboids and cylinders. They will be taught how to measure the perimeters, areas and volumes of shapes.

Handling data
Data is simply information, in this case mainly numbers. Your child will be taught how to collect, sort, display and interpret this information.

■ WHAT YOUR CHILD WILL STUDY
From five to seven
In the infants, the approach to *using and applying mathematics* will be based on practical activities drawn from the other areas of mathematical work. So, for example, children might be asked to sort and classify in different ways a number of coloured shapes, e.g. by length. Or they might learn how to use a balance to compare the weight of different objects. They would then be encouraged to make predictions about the weight of other objects based on their findings so far. They will be encouraged to talk about their findings and to give reasons why they think, for example, a larger object will be heavier than a small one. Children will also start to learn how to apply mathematics to 'real life'. So, they might learn how to measure a table, using their own handspans.

In their *number* work, children of five or six should be able to count up to ten using objects, such as bricks. Still using objects or counters, they should be able to add and subtract with numbers up to 10. They should also be able to make a sensible estimate of any number of objects up to 10.

As they progress they should – by the age of six or seven – be using and ordering numbers up to at least 10. The most able children will be able to use numbers up to 1000 and be capable of subtraction and addition up to 20. They will also be doing simple multiplication, and will learn their 2, 5 and 10 multiplication tables. They might approach number work through the use of money, adding up costs and working out what change to give. They should also be introduced to the meaning of 'half' and 'quarter'.

In *algebra*, the youngest children will begin by learning about pattern in numbers or objects. So they might learn how to complete a number pattern, such as: 1,1,2,1,1,2 – – –. They should learn how to distinguish between odd and even numbers and – as they progress – learn that a symbol can stand for an unknown number.

For their work on *shape and space* the youngest pupils should be learning how to sort and classify two- and three-dimensional shapes. Older children – at six or seven – should be introduced to a wider variety of shapes, including rectangles, pentagons, spheres etc. As they progress, they should begin to understand about angles and to recognise a right-angle. They will be using units of measurement for length, weight and capacity. They might also be learning about compass bearings and terms like 'clockwise' and 'anticlockwise'.

The first steps towards *handling data* will involve collecting and recording information, for example from a questionnaire about how children get to school, using graphs and diagrams to represent the frequency of use of each form of transport.

These different aspects of mathematics – although separated here for ease of explanation – are likely to be combined into single projects. So, for example, children might be asked by their teacher to take their teddy-bears to school. These can then be used for a number of mathematical activities, for example:

★ counting the bears and the number of arms/legs they have.
★ answering questions, such as 'Which is the tallest?'.
★ sorting the bears in order of size.
★ arranging bears in different families and other groupings according to size, colour, shape.

From seven to eleven
In the juniors, children's work on *using and applying mathematics* will continue to involve them in choosing practical materials to carry out tasks. But by this stage there will be more opportunities for choice in the way problems are approached, for example planning alternative layouts for the desks and other furniture in the classroom. Put simply, this means they must find different ways of reaching a solution. They will be set tasks which require them to test the truth of statements such as 'it is harder to get a 6 when throwing dice than to get a 1'.

In their *number* work, children will be building on their work in the infants, but moving towards bigger numbers. They should be able to do sums in their heads and on paper, using two- and three-digit numbers. They will continue to learn all their multiplication tables.

They should also be improving their knowledge of simple fractions. This might involve estimating how full a bottle is or cutting a piece of string into halves or quarters. The decimal point is also introduced at this stage. So pupils should be learning that three pound coins and six pennies can be recorded as '£3.06' or how to read and record measurements to two decimal points (e.g. 3.45 kg). At this stage, they will also be doing activities to familiarise themselves with simple percentages.

For their work on *shape and space*, the younger children should be recognising reflective symmetry in a variety of two- and three-dimensional shapes. They should be able to construct for themselves simple two- and three-dimensional shapes and should be using the language of angles, such as 'acute', 'obtuse' and 'reflex'. They will be finding out how to measure areas by counting squares and volumes by counting cubes. Towards the top end of the junior school, the more able children will be measuring and drawing angles and using the formulae for finding the areas of squares, rectangles, triangles and circles.

Finally, for their work on *handling data* younger children might work on gathering information such as the height and date of birth of children in the class. This can then be used to construct and interpret bar charts and graphs, for example showing how many children have their birthdays in each month. They will be introduced to 'mean', 'mode' and 'median'. They will also start to use collected information to make estimates of probabilities and will learn to handle data using computers.

From 11 to 14

In secondary school, pupils will be given the chance to demonstrate greater sophistication in *using and applying mathematics*. So they might, for example, collect different types of charts, diagrams and graphs from newspapers or other published reports which show different ways of representing numerical information. Then they would be encouraged to ask whether these methods are misleading or open to misinterpretation. They might be asked to come up with different ways of presenting the information. As they move towards the end of the age group, they might be asked to design a task to solve a practical problem, such as working out the relationship between arm-span and height.

In their *number* work, pupils in the early years of secondary school will be building on the mental arithmetic work they began at primary school, using larger numbers. There will also be pencil-and-paper work without the use of pocket calculators, i.e. multiplication and division of multi-digit numbers. They should also be starting to work with negative numbers. With calculators, pupils should be calculating fractions and percentages and using estimation and approximation to check if their answers are likely to be correct.

In *algebra*, pupils should be learning number patterns in multiplication and division. For example, they will be finding out that these are inverse operations and will use this to check calculations. They should be plotting points and graphs in the first quadrant (i.e. the area within the positive axes, most commonly used for simple graphs). Older or more able pupils will be using spreadsheets or other computer facilities to explore number patterns. They will also be using simple formulae or equations written in symbolic form.

In their studies of *space and shape*, younger pupils will be continuing their earlier work on two- and three-dimensional shapes, sorting them and recognising their angles and their symmetry. They will become familiar with specifying locations on maps through grid references. As they progress they will move on to locating points within the four quadrants. They will be learning how to work out perimeters, areas and volumes.

While *handling data*, pupils in this age group will be making more detailed use of a computer database. They will collect, order and group data, for example from their experiments in science, geography or technology. This might include using pie charts, conversion graphs, frequency diagrams, and scatter graphs.

From 14 to 16
At 14 pupils begin their GCSE courses which are currently being adapted to ensure they fit in with the requirements of the National Curriculum.

By now – in *using and applying mathematics* – youngsters will be following alternative lines of investigation, selecting different mathematical methods to find solutions to real-life tasks. They will be learning how to work methodically, making detailed plans and checking their results.

Number work at this stage becomes more complex as pupils move on to working out more difficult calculations using both mental arithmetic and calculators. They will also learn how to work out percentage changes and recognise the equivalence of fractions.

In *algebra*, pupils will be solving simple equations, exploring complex number patterns generated by a computer, and using a range of formulae.

In their work on *shape and space*, they will be calculating the lengths, areas and volumes of a wide variety of shapes. They will be devising instructions for computers to generate and transform two-dimensional shapes. They will learn about Pythagoras' theorem (that the square on the hypotenuse of a right-angled triangle is equal to the sum of the squares on the two other sides). Towards the end of this age group they may also be calculating the surface area of cylinders and the volumes of cones and spheres.

In *data handling*, they will work on ways of testing a simple hypothesis, designing questionnaires, collecting and analysing results. They should be doing more complex calculations involving the mean, median, mode, and range of frequency distribution for sets of data.

■ WHAT YOUR CHILD IS EXPECTED TO KNOW
At seven
Children will take their first formal, nationally-set tests in mathematics at the end of the infant school, when most of them will be seven. The new tests – known as Standard Assessment Tasks, or SATs – will cover basic number work, such as sums. Children will be tested on their mental arithmetic as well as on calculations done with pencil and paper and with a calculator. The former involves the teacher reading out a list of about a dozen additions and subtractions using numbers up to 10, with pupils given five seconds to write down each answer. (See page 69 for more details.) There will also be tests of either children's ability in handling numerical data or their grasp of probability. Other aspects of mathematics will be assessed during normal classwork by your child's own teacher.

At this age, if your child is progressing at the average rate they should be at *Level Two* on the National Curriculum ten-point scale. However, more able pupils will be tested to see if they have reached either *Level Three* (the average level for nine year-olds) or even *Level Four* (the average level for pupils at 11).

To reach *Level Two*, your child will be expected, amongst other things, to be able to do the following:

★ make no more than one mistake in addition and one in subtraction during a mental arithmetic test using numbers up to 10.

★ understand and work with numbers up to 100, using pencil and paper for calculations.

★ simple addition and subtraction using numbers up to 10, for example working out the change from 20p when two items costing 5p and 7p are purchased.

★ understand the meaning of 'half' and 'quarter', for example knowing that 4 is half of 8.

★ make a sensible estimate of a number of objects up to 20.

★ solve simple algebra problems, such as $3 + x = 10$.

★ recognise squares, rectangles, circles, triangles, hexagons, pentagons, cubes, cuboids, cylinders, and spheres.

★ understand the notion of 'angle', and recognise right-angles.

★ know about common measurements, such as metres, miles, litres, pints, pounds.

To reach *Level Three*, your child should – amongst other things – be able to do the following:

★ understand numbers up to 1000.

★ addition and subtraction using numbers up to 20.

★ know the 2, 5 and 10 times table.

★ multiplication up to 5×5, for example, how many cakes costing 5p each can you buy for 20p?

★ solve more difficult calculations using an electronic calculator, e.g. the cost of four books at £2.25 each.

★ understand the meaning of negative numbers.

★ continue number patterns using two-digit numbers, such as 5, 10, 15, 20. . . .

★ understand the eight points of the compass, e.g. North, North-East, East, South-East.

★ understand 'clockwise' and 'anticlockwise'.

★ understand symmetry in objects.

★ construct simple bar charts and graphs.

At eleven

At the end of primary school, your child will take the second lot of nationally-set tests in mathematics. As at seven, the written tests – or SATs – will cover only some aspects of mathematics. Others will be assessed by teachers on the basis of normal classroom work.

An 11-year-old of average ability should have reached *Level Four* on the ten-point scale. More able pupils may already be at *Level Five or Six* which is the average for a 14-year-old.

To reach *Level Four*, pupils should, amongst other things, be able to do the following:

★ know multiplication tables up to 10×10.

★ mentally add or subtract two-digit numbers, e.g. $37 + 42$.

★ add and subtract three-digit numbers using pencil-and-paper, but not a calculator.

★ understand decimal places and the effect of multiplication by 10 or 100.

★ use fractions and percentages, e.g. knowing that 9 out of 100 books represents 9 per cent.

★ plot points using co-ordinates in the first quadrant.

★ find places on a map using grid references.

★ conduct a survey, collecting and interpreting the results, for example the number of pupils born in each month of the year.

At fourteen

By the time your child takes the third nationally-set tests they should have reached the average level for 14-year-olds, which is about half-way between *Level Five* and *Level Six* on the ten-point scale.

The current plan is for 14-year-olds to take three one-hour written tests covering number, algebra, shape and space, and the handling of numerical data. The other aspect of the subject – using and applying mathematics – will be assessed by teachers during normal classwork.

To reach *Level Five*, pupils should, amongst other things, be able to do the following:

★ mental arithmetic such as 70×500 or 800 divided by 20.

★ pencil and paper calculations using two- and three-digit numbers, such as working out the number of coaches needed to take 167 people on an outing when each coach has 42 seats.

★ work out fractions and percentages using a calculator, e.g. 15 per cent of £320.

★ understand negative numbers, e.g. work out the temperature change from $-4°$ celsius to $+20°$.

★ convert metric units to Imperial units still in use, e.g. 1 kg is about 2.2lb or 1 litre is about 1.75 pints.

★ understand and use such terms as: prime, square, square root, multiple and factor.

★ measure and draw angles to the nearest degree.
★ know and use the formulae for finding the areas of squares, triangles, rectangles and circles.

To reach *Level Six*, your child should – amongst other things – be able to do the following:
★ work out fractional and percentage changes, e.g. the saving involved in a 15 per cent discount.
★ use ratios to adapt from one situation to another, e.g. adapting a recipe for 6 people to one for 8.
★ understand the equivalance of fractions, e.g. $2/5 = 4/10 = 0.4 = 40$ per cent.
★ use estimation to check calculations, e.g. that 278 divided by 39 is about 7.
★ solve relatively simple equations, such as $3y + 4 = 10 - y$ (answer: $y = 1.5$).
★ use bearings to describe the position of a ship or aircraft.

At sixteen

The final nationally-set tests in the National Curriculum take place when most pupils are 16. This will be in the form of GCSEs, which are being adapted so that from 1994 the current A to G grades will be translated into levels 10 to 4 on the National Curriculum scale.

The average 16 year-old should have reached half-way between *Level Six* and *Level Seven*. This will be roughly equal to a grade D at GCSE. Abler pupils may have reached level Eight (GCSE grade B) or even Level Nine or Ten (GCSE grade A).

To reach *Level Seven* (C/D at GCSE), pupils should – amongst other things – be able to:
★ do mental arithmetic, such as 80×0.2 or $600 \div 0.2$.
★ use a calculator to convert inches to centimetres given that there are 0.394 inches to the centimetre.
★ solve equations such as $2x - y = 9$ and $x + 3y = 8$ (answer: $x = 5$ and $y = 1$).
★ use graphs to solve distance/time problems.
★ use coordinates to locate position in three dimensions.
★ calculate the length of one side of a right-angled triangle when the other two sides are known, using Pythagoras' theorem.

To reach *Level Nine* (equivalent to GCSE grade A) or *Ten* (grade A+), pupils should amongst other things be able to:
★ distinguish between rational and irrational numbers and the difference between recurring and non-recurring decimals.

★ work out velocity in distance/time graphs and acceleration in velocity/time graphs.

★ use diagrams, graphs and computer packages to analyse a set of complex data.

★ solve problems in two dimensions, e.g. the collision point of two ships moving at constant speeds on different courses.

★ solve problems in three dimensions, e.g. the transformation of shapes.

★ calculate the probability of any two events happening, e.g. getting a 'five' and 'heads' when tossing a dice and a coin simultaneously.

8
SCIENCE

■

WHAT DOES SCIENCE INVOLVE?

WHAT WILL MY CHILD STUDY?

WHAT WILL MY CHILD BE EXPECTED TO KNOW?

■ WHAT DOES SCIENCE INVOLVE?

Science is one of the three core subjects. That means your child must take the subject from the age of five right up to 16, ending for all pupils with a course leading to either one or two GCSEs. Virtually all pupils will take the GCSE examination.

Aspects of sex education are part of the compulsory science course. In the juniors, they will learn about reproduction in both plants and mammals and will be introduced to the idea of genetic inheritance. In the early years at secondary school, they will be taught the physical and emotional changes that occur in adolescence and about the need to have a responsible attitude to sexual behaviour. They will also learn about AIDS and the HIV virus.

Health education also falls under the science umbrella. In the infants, they will learn about the importance of personal hygiene and how to keep healthy through exercise. In the juniors they should go into more detail, learning about the safe handling of food and about dental care. They will also be told about harmful drugs and about the risks from alcohol and tobacco.

The introduction of science to children under 11 is one of the biggest changes brought about by the National Curriculum. In the past, it was estimated that primary schools devoted only around 5 per cent of teaching time to science. Many primary schools say they are still short of the space and equipment required for National Curriculum science and many primary teachers have very little expertise in science.

At the primary stage science does not conform to the traditional image of complicated experiments in laboratories. Instead it is about encouraging children to be curious about the world around them and to begin to do simple experiments to find out about the properties of materials, light, sound, magnetism and so on. Although it is now compulsory, science will not always be taught as a separate subject to younger children. Instead it may be taught through topics such as flight, energy or food which can combine work on other subjects at the same time.

In secondary school, science will usually appear as a separate subject on the timetable. However, the National Curriculum does not follow the traditional separation of science into physics, chemistry and biology. Instead all three are covered by 'balanced science'. This approach has been supported by the two main head teachers' associations who say balanced science covers all the essential knowledge of the three separate sciences and will ensure that all youngsters get a broad scientific education.

However, some independent schools objected to the balanced science approach and are exercising their freedom to continue teaching physics, chemistry and biology separately. But many independent school head teachers do admit the advantages of balanced science. Vivian Anthony, secretary of the Headmasters' Conference, believes the combined subject is particularly appropriate for giving a broad foundation in science to those pupils who are unlikely to continue with science subjects after 16.

It is still possible for pupils in state schools as well as private schools to take separate GCSEs in physics, chemistry, and biology if they wish. If pupils do opt for separate science subjects then they must take all three, not just one or two. From 1994 onwards the more common approach will be for pupils to take a GCSE in balanced science. Students taking the full National Curriculum course up to the age of 16 will take a 'double' award, worth two GCSEs. Other students who want to do less science between the ages of 14 and 16 will take a 'single' award, worth one GCSE.

If your children take the double science option they will spend around one-fifth of their timetable doing science. Single science will occupy only around one-eighth of their time. The head teachers' associations have recommended that as many youngsters as possible take the full option, which must be available in all schools. However they accept that the narrower course may be better suited to youngsters who show little interest in science or are having difficulty keeping up.

National Curriculum science is divided into four main areas:

Scientific investigation
Life and living processes
Materials and their properties } *Scientific knowledge*
Physical processes

Scientific investigation is about developing the skills needed to find out about the natural and scientific world. It involves learning to observe, investigate and carry out experiments. Pupils will be taught how to measure, record and interpret their findings. This aspect of science is considered particularly important at primary school.

Life and living processes covers all living things: human, animal and plant life. This includes inheritance, selection and evolution and the way different organisms survive within particular habitats.

Materials and their properties covers the study of rocks, minerals and soils and other types of materials. Pupils will learn about chemical reactions and the theories which explain the properties of particular types of materials.

Physical processes covers the study of energy and forces, including gravity and magnetism. Pupils will also learn about light, sound and electricity and will find out about the solar system and the Universe.

■ WHAT YOUR CHILD WILL STUDY
From five to seven

In *scientific investigation* children might, for example, be asked to find out whether different objects float or sink, carrying out experiments with different objects, such as wood, feathers, stones, and fruit. They will learn how to record their findings in chart form. Then – working from these results – they will be asked to explain why some things sink and others float, and to predict what will happen with other objects.

Using different types of experiment, children will learn how to describe, sort and group objects, making notes on their similarities and differences. They will learn how to measure objects, for example in terms of their own hand-spans or foot-lengths. They will weigh objects, perhaps using marbles as measuring weights. When recording their findings, they should try out different methods of showing results, deciding for example whether a block graph or a frequency chart is more appropriate.

As they start to build up their *scientific knowledge* children will usually start by finding out about themselves. They will be taught about how people grow, need food to survive, how they move and use

---

SCIENCE ACTIVITIES FOR FIVE TO SEVEN-YEAR-OLDS
- sorting, grouping and describing objects.
- doing experiments, then recording and interpreting the results.
- measuring and weighing objects or each other.
- learning about humans, animals and plants.
- observing and recording the weather.
- collecting natural objects found in the area, such as rocks, wood, soil.
- discovering how materials change when heated, dissolved, squashed or twisted.
- learning about forces which pull, push, and stop objects.
- learning about electricity, light and sound.

---

their senses and about the main stages in their development from baby to adult. They will also learn about the importance of exercise, diet, personal hygiene, rest and personal safety.

At this age they will also learn about other forms of life, in the animal and plant worlds. They will be taught that some life-forms are extinct. Dinosaurs are always a popular example. They should learn how plants grow, feed and reproduce, studying nearby habitats such as the school playing-field or nature area, their own gardens, or local ponds or woods.

There is also a 'green' element to the infant school science curriculum. Children are expected to look at how people change the local environment by their activities. They should look at the rubbish we throw away and learn to sort things into those that decay and those that do not. They should be encouraged to work out for themselves how to improve their immediate surroundings.

In learning to observe their local natural environment, they should be given the chance to collect and study natural and man-made objects such as rocks, air, water and other liquids. They will also be introduced to the idea that some objects can change their shape and form when cooled or heated, for example ice, water, wax or chocolate. They will also learn that other objects change permanently when heated e.g. bread or wood.

Children are also introduced to electricity and its uses in the classroom and at home. They will be doing simple activities with buzzers, bulbs, batteries and wires and discovering that some materials conduct electricity while others do not. Sound and light are also covered at this stage. They should learn about ways to make sounds,

SCIENCE PROJECTS IN PRIMARY SCHOOLS

Weather
- describing different kinds of weather.
- making rainfall or sunshine frequency charts.
- collecting and measuring rainfall.
- listening to weather forecasts.
- discussing why we need different types of weather.
- observing how the weather affects plants, crops, trees.
- noting how the weather makes us hot/cold/wet.
- learning about weather in other countries (floods, droughts, hurricanes).

Animals and Plants
- investigating a habitat such as a playing field, a garden, river or pond.
- recording what grows where and devising ways of recording this.
- grouping plants by common characteristics.
- making interpretations (e.g. why grass grows longer in some areas).
- examining plants and learning about seeds.
- finding out what insect or animal life occurs in the habitat.
- discussing the difference between an animal and a plant.
- finding out how plants, insects and larger animals need each other.

Food
- comparing the food we eat here with that eaten in different countries.
- finding out where our food comes from.
- learning why we need different kinds of food to stay healthy (vitamins, proteins etc).
- measuring and weighing food.
- finding out how diet has changed over the years.
- learning how food is preserved.
- learning about farming, and perhaps visiting a farm.

using familiar objects and simple musical instruments. Similarly, with light they should learn about various sources of light and about shadows, reflection and colour. They will learn about forces by lifting, pushing and pulling objects. They will also learn how forces work in wind-up or electrically driven toys.

At this age, your child will be introduced to science mainly through projects. Teachers have freedom to select the topics they think best. Often schools will encourage the help of parents – or at the very least ask you to supply necessary objects! Do encourage your child to tell you what projects they are working on. Then you can discuss and encourage further exploration in these areas at home or on family visits. Some of the projects schools might use to teach aspects of the science curriculum are listed on the previous page.

From seven to eleven

As children move on to junior school, they will be taught to take a more systematic and detailed approach to their *scientific investigation*. So they might use, for example, digital watches to time experiments. They will also make greater use of computers. Instead of being told what to measure and how to do it, increasingly they will be expected to decide for themselves. From their results, they will learn how to devise general principles and hypotheses and then go on to test these.

The *scientific knowledge* they will cover is now much broader, going beyond what is easily observable in their everyday life. So investigation spreads out from the local environment to study of the night sky, and finding out about the sun, moon and Earth. They will also look more closely at how forces work, using examples from everyday life such as cycling or sailing and hydraulic mechanisms.

These are just a few of the things your child will be learning about at this age:

Life and living processes
★ an introduction to the major organs of mammals and flowering plants.
★ the basic processes of breathing, circulation, growth and reproduction.
★ factors that influence the rate of plant growth (light intensity, temperature, and the amount of fertiliser).
★ the body's defence systems and the effects of bacteria on health.
★ learning about at least two different habitats and the animals and plants that live there.
★ the effects of farming, mining and industry on the environment and the effects of pollution.

Materials and their properties
★ how sands, soils, and rocks are affected by the weather.

★ what happens when materials are heated and cooled.

★ the properties of everyday materials, such as weight, volume, strength, solubility.

★ tests for acidity or alkalinity.

★ exploring chemical changes in everyday materials e.g. plaster of Paris, mixing concrete, firing clay.

★ techniques for separating mixtures such as muddy water, sea water, ink (i.e. evaporation, filtration etc).

Physical processes

★ studying models driven by motors, belts, levers and gears.

★ friction and its effects on moving objects.

★ construction of simple electrical circuits and the dangers of electricity.

★ the properties of magnetic and non-magnetic materials.

★ how sound is made and how changes in pitch and loudness are made by changing the length, tension or thickness of a vibrating object.

★ how light passes through lenses, prisms, filters.

★ learning about the movements of the Earth, moon and sun and the causes of day and night, eclipses and the seasons of the year.

From 11 to 14

In secondary school, pupils will be using much more sophisticated equipment in their *scientific investigation*. They will be expected to plan their own experiments and to use increasingly complex instruments to take measurements. They will learn how to search for patterns in complicated data and how to use computers.

The range of *scientific knowledge* really mushrooms by this stage and much of it will start to be beyond the comprehension of non-scientific parents. Be prepared for difficult questions! The following are just a few of the areas that must be covered.

Life and living processes

★ life processes, such as feeding, respiration, growth and reproduction.

★ photosynthesis in green plants.

★ the human life cycle, including the physical and emotional changes of adolescence and the need to have a responsible attitude to sexual behaviour.

★ genetic inheritance.

★ factors affecting the size of populations of organisms, such as competition for resources and predation.
★ the classifications of biodegradable and non-biodegradable matter.

Materials and their properties
★ the water cycle and how airstreams affect the weather.
★ energy from the sun, nuclear energy, fossil fuels.
★ how to classify metals, ceramics, glass, plastics and fibres.
★ the difference between elements, compounds and mixtures.
★ types of reactions, such as combustion, oxidation, electrolysis and fermentation.

Physical processes
★ how simple machines and tools such as pulleys and levers work.
★ the measurement of speed and its relationship to stopping distance.
★ the use of more complicated electrical devices, such as potentiometers, relays and switches.
★ uses of electric motors, dynamos, transformers, loudspeakers and fuses.
★ how the ear works and common defects of hearing.
★ the behaviour of light, including absorption, reflection, refraction and dispersion.
★ the position of the solar system in the Universe.

From 14 to 16
At this age, pupils must decide whether or not to continue with the full science course worth two GCSEs or to opt for a reduced course, worth just one. The full course is recommended for the majority of pupils, and certainly for anyone intending to continue with science after 16.

On both courses pupils will be taught to continue developing skills of *scientific investigation*. By now they are expected to deal in increasingly abstract concepts and to show greater invention and creativity in their exploration. They will make greater use of computers in their scientific research and are expected to record and display information in more detail.

Both courses cover physics, chemistry and biology. The *scientific knowledge* covered by the full course includes, amongst other things, the following:

Life and living processes
★ the major organ systems and life processes and how behaviour relates to survival and reproduction.
★ how hormones can control and promote fertility and growth.
★ DNA and how it determines cell function.
★ ideas of evolution, selective breeding and cloning.
★ a detailed study of a locality.
★ the effect of human activity on pollution (e.g. the use of fertilisers).

Materials and their properties
★ the principles which govern the behaviour of gases in the atmosphere.
★ atmospheric circulation, including the relationship between pressure, winds and weather patterns.
★ the economic and environmental implications of using different energy sources, including looking at the 'greenhouse effect'.
★ how to classify materials as solids, liquids and gases.
★ how to represent chemical and electrolytic reactions in symbolic equations.
★ the processes involved in metal extraction, cracking oil (decomposing heavy oils into lighter hydrocarbons such as petrol), the chloralkali industry and the production of plastics and fertilisers.

Physical processes
★ investigating the relationship between forces, work and power through devices for doing work, including the human body.
★ the study of electrical circuits and the measurements of voltage and current.
★ the fundamental characteristics of sound, including loudness, amplitude, pitch and frequency.
★ understanding a wave model, e.g. by observing waves on water and relating this to sound waves.
★ the fundamental characteristics of light, including reflection, refraction, diffraction, interference and polarisation.
★ understanding past and present ideas to explain the character and origin of the Earth, other planets, stars and the universe.

■ WHAT YOUR CHILD IS EXPECTED TO KNOW
At primary school, great emphasis is placed on pupils' skills in scientific investigation. So it has been recommended that this area

should be worth 50 per cent of marks in tests and assessments, with the other 50 per cent shared between the other three areas. In the secondary school, each of the four areas will carry equal weight.

At seven
When children are tested at seven, there will be both nationally-set Standard Assessment Tasks and assessments made by the class teacher over a longer period. The SATs will cover either *materials* or *Earth and atmosphere*. (See page 70 for more details.)

The child of average ability is expected to be at *Level Two* on the National Curriculum ten-point scale. To achieve that, they should, among other things, be able to do or know the following:

Scientific investigation
★ ask and answer questions of the 'how', 'why', and 'what will happen if . . .' variety.
★ explain why a toy car travels further on a smooth surface than on a rough one.
★ make deductions from experiments such as 'light objects float', 'heavy objects sink', 'thin wood is bendy', 'thick wood does not bend'.

Life and living processes
★ know that living things need food, water and air to survive.
★ know that all humans are unique.
★ classify materials into things which decay naturally (e.g. fruit peel) and those which do not (plastics and tin cans).

Materials and their properties
★ group materials according to their physical characteristics.
★ know that heating and cooling everyday materials can cause them to melt or solidify or change permanently.

Physical processes
★ understand the meaning of hot and cold and how to use a thermometer.
★ know that Earth, moon, and sun are separate spherical bodies.
★ understand that pushes and pulls can make things start moving, speed up, swerve, stop or change shape.
★ know that magnets attract some materials and not others.
★ know that light passes through some materials and not others and how shadows are formed.

At eleven

The second formal National Curriculum tests are taken at the end of primary school, when the majority of children are eleven. By this age, the child of average ability is expected to be at around *Level Four* on the National Curriculum ten-point scale. To achieve this, they should be able to do or know the following:

Scientific investigation
★ suggest testable ideas based on some prior knowledge and under-standing, for example 'all objects fall, but heavy objects fall fastest'.
★ carry out a fair test to prove this.
★ use appropriate instruments for measuring things.

Life and living processes
★ name and locate the major organs of the human body and flowering plants.
★ identify animals as mammals, birds, reptiles, amphibians and fish.
★ understand that plants and animals compete for resources to survive.
★ understand food chains such as rose bush – greenfly – ladybird – blue tit.

Materials and their properties
★ know how movements of air and water in the atmosphere affect the weather.
★ understand how weathering and transport of rocks create different types of soil.
★ recognise the basic qualities of solids, liquids and gases.
★ recognise that materials can be changed into different forms, such as wood into charcoal or dough into bread.

Physical processes
★ recognise that the solar system is made up of the sun and planets, and have an idea of its scale.
★ explain day/night and length of day in terms of the movement of the Earth around the sun.
★ design and make a circuit for a working model, including a motor or a buzzer.
★ be able to construct simple electrical circuits from diagrams.
★ know that light travels faster than sound.
★ know that light travels in straight lines.

At fourteen

The third set of formal tests are taken by pupils when the majority in their class are 14. The current plan is for three one-hour written tests covering each of the areas below, except scientific investigation (which will be assessed by class teachers).

Pupils of average ability should be at around *Level Five or Six* on the National Curriculum ten-point scale. To achieve this, some of the things they should know or be able to do include:

Scientific investigation
★ make suppositions involving cause and effect based on scientific theory (e.g. that more sugar will dissolve in hot water than in the same amount of cold water because temperature increases solubility).
★ observe with greater accuracy and detail (e.g. reading minor divisions on thermometers).
★ understand that different interpretations are possible from experiments.

Life and living processes
★ the functions of the major organ systems in flowering plants and mammals.
★ that information in the form of genes is passed on from one generation to the next.
★ how pollution can affect the survival of organisms.
★ that the key factors in the process of decay are temperature, microbes, moisture and air.

Materials and their properties
★ how the water cycle works.
★ how to classify aqueous solutions as acidic, alkaline, or neutral using pH.
★ how to separate and purify mixtures (such as muddy or salty water) by filtration, dissolving or evaporation.

Physical processes
★ the difference between renewable (e.g. wind or wave power) and non-renewable (coal or oil) energy.
★ be able to explain that the solar system forms part of a galaxy which is part of a larger system called the universe.
★ the ues of switches, relays, potentiometers and logic gates in controlling simple circuits.

★ the rule governing the reflection of light at plane surfaces.
★ the relationship between an applied force, the area over which it acts and the resulting pressure.

At sixteen

The National Curriculum comes to an end with GCSE examinations which are taken by most students when they are 16. The final two years of the National Curriculum course are married with GCSE syllabuses. The grades of the GCSE are being adapted to the ten-level scale of the National Curriculum and from 1994 students will be graded from Four (lowest) to Ten (highest), rather than G to A. Levels One to Three do not achieve a GCSE grade.

The 16-year-old of average ability should be at around *Level Six or Seven* by the time of the GCSE examinations. This is roughly equal to a GCSE grade of C, D or E. To achieve this, some of the things pupils should know or be able to do include:

Scientific investigation
★ carry out investigations involving several variables and formulate hypotheses involving relationships between those variables (e.g. the factors affecting the rate of photosynthesis).
★ make observations involving fine discrimination and use highly detailed measuring instruments.
★ interpret data on a graph to give values outside the range collected, for example by extrapolation and interpolation.

Life and living processes
★ understand that animals and plants adapt their size, shape and behaviour to their natural environment in order to survive.
★ know that living organisms change through both genetic and environmental causes.
★ understand the relationships between population change and environmental resources.
★ understand the economic benefits of selective breeding.

Materials and their properties
★ the scientific processes which form igneous, sedimentary and metamorphic rocks.
★ explain the physical differences between solids, liquids, and gases in simple particle terms (e.g. that particles are held together strongly in ice cubes but less strongly in water).

★ how to recognise the variations in the properties of metals.
★ the factors which influence the rate of a chemical reaction.
★ the difference between elements, compounds and mixtures in terms of atoms, ions and molecules.

Physical processes
★ the qualitative relationships between force, distance, work, power and time.
★ the magnetic effect of an electric current and its use in electromagnets.
★ the relationship between current, voltage and resistance.
★ how energy is transferred thermally in solids, liquids, gases and a vacuum.

To reach *Level Nine* (equivalent to GCSE grade A) or *Ten* (grade A+), pupils should amongst other things be able to:

Scientific investigation
★ use scientific theory to make predictions.
★ use scientific knowledge and an understanding of laws, theories and models to develop hypotheses explaining the behaviour of objects.

Life and living processes
★ explain the coordination of the body's activities through nervous and hormonal control.
★ understand the basic scientific principles associated with a major change in the biosphere (i.e. the earth's crust and atmosphere where living matter is found).
★ understand the basic principles of genetic engineering, selective breeding and cloning and the social and ethical issues these raise.

Materials and their properties
★ explain atmospheric changes that cause weather phenomena.
★ explain the layered structure of the inner Earth.
★ understand the theory of plate tectonics.

Physical processes
★ evaluate the economic, environmental and social benefits of different energy sources.
★ understand the principles of electromagnetic induction.
★ understand the concept of momentum and its conservation.

9
FOREIGN LANGUAGES
■

WHAT DO FOREIGN LANGUAGES INVOLVE?
WHAT WILL MY CHILD STUDY?
WHAT WILL MY CHILD BE EXPECTED TO KNOW?

■ **WHAT DO FOREIGN LANGUAGES INVOLVE?**

Learning a foreign language has never been more important than now. For today's pupils it will be an invaluable skill. The creation of the Single European Market and the building of the Channel Tunnel will mean closer business and social ties with the rest of Europe. Employers will increasingly want staff who can speak foreign languages and there will be greater job opportunities for people wishing to cross European borders to find work. As well as being of practical use, learning a language can be great fun in itself and it leads to greater knowledge of other countries and cultures.

It is often said that the British are either too lazy or – as an island race – unsuited to be linguists. But the experts who devised the languages curriculum insist there is no such thing as a national inability to learn foreign languages. Despite the world-wide use of English, they say the new curriculum should help ensure that the Briton who is unable to speak even one foreign language will become an increasingly rare species.

The new curriculum requires all youngsters to study at least one modern foreign language from the age of 11 until 16. From the age of 14 pupils may, if their school offers the choice, do a 'short course' in a foreign language. They may be able to combine this with another short course such as geography or with a subject from outside the National Curriculum, such as business studies. It has not yet been decided which qualifications these would lead to, but it could be either a GCSE, an equivalent vocational qualification or some new qualification altogether.

Many people are disappointed that – unlike all the other National Curriculum subjects – modern foreign languages are not compulsory in primary schools. Since children of this age are now required to study other subjects like science and technology, the timetable is already very full and primary schools which have been teaching French up to now may feel they have to drop it. Language experts say there is no reason why primary school children cannot learn a foreign language, particularly now there is more emphasis on practical, spoken language rather than just the written language. A more serious obstacle is the lack of primary school teachers with foreign language expertise.

Does it have to be French?

Although French is the language most commonly taught, some schools may offer different languages. All schools must offer at least one European Community language, but they can also offer any others from a list of 19 languages. In practice most schools will only be able to teach a small selection of languages because of the availability of teachers.

The full list of options is as follows:

Arabic
This is one of the six official languages of the United Nations and the language of the Koran. It is written from right to left in a form of shorthand.

Bengali
This is one of the official languages in India and is the official language of Bangladesh.

Chinese
There is a choice of either of the two most important of China's spoken languages: Mandarin and Cantonese. The former is designated as the national language of China.

Danish
This is the mother tongue of only around five million people, but it is regarded as a bridge to learning other Scandinavian and Nordic languages.

Dutch
As a language of Germanic origins, Dutch has many similarities with other European languages, including English.

French

This is the first foreign language experienced by most pupils. It is particularly useful not only as the language of our nearest Continental neighbour, but also as one of the official languages of the European Community. It is spoken by an estimated 120 million people across the world.

German

Like French, this is a tremendously useful language, particularly in the light of the changes in eastern Europe where it is widely spoken and understood.

Greek

This is the modern language, not the classical language from which it derives. Greek terminology influences many modern languages, particularly in medicine and science.

Gujarati

This is one of the official languages of India and the language of the Indian State of Gujarat.

Hebrew

Modern Hebrew is the official language of the State of Israel and is spoken by Jewish communities around the world.

Hindi

This is the national language of India and is widely understood by Indians who have other mother tongues.

Italian

It is only fairly recently that standard Italian has started to replace local dialects. It has the advantage of being a very melodic language.

Japanese

Perhaps surprisingly, Japanese does not cause great pronunciation difficulties for most people. In view of the economic power of Japan – and the arrival of several big Japanese companies in Britain – it is a very useful language.

Panjabi

This is the official language of the Panjab state in India and many Panjabi speakers have emigrated to Britain.

Portuguese

This is the national language of both Portugal and Brazil and variants are spoken in former Portuguese colonies in Africa, Asia, and India.

Russian

As the official language of the former Soviet Union, Russian will continue to be widely understood throughout the Soviet commonwealth whatever political developments occur in future.

Spanish
Spanish is very widely spoken throughout the world, and the number of speakers is growing. Although there are wide variations – even in Spain itself – from the Castilian version it is widely understood by speakers of other versions such as Catalan.

Turkish
As well as being the national language of Turkey, this is also spoken by many people living in Yugoslavia, Bulgaria, Greece and Cyprus.

Urdu
Urdu is a commonly understood language throughout the Indian sub-continent. It is the mother tongue of several million people in India and in Pakistan where it is the official language.

Although French remains the most common foreign language, there are signs that – where they are available – Spanish and German are very popular as a first-choice language. Although it is not required by the new curriculum, some schools continue to encourage pupils to take more than one foreign language. Usually this has only been available for more able pupils, but many believe it should be more widespread. In many of our neighbouring European countries it is common for children to learn more than one foreign language at a fairly young age.

Experts say the best way to teach a foreign language is to speak that language as much as possible in the classroom. Even in the early years at secondary school, it is quite possible for teachers to speak only French or German to pupils from the moment they enter the classroom to the time they leave it. They also agree that children respond best if lessons and vocabulary relate as far as possible to their own interests (learning the vocabulary of different colours in relation to soccer club shirts, for example).

Some of the best teaching I have seen involved putting youngsters in 'real life' situations. In Havering in Essex, for example, the education authority has set up a simulated continental village. Local schools can visit the Europa Centre in Hornchurch and experience a day-trip to France or Germany. The day begins with passport control and includes visits to shops, restaurants and cafés. No English is spoken. Street and shop signs revolve and can be changed from French to German according to the language the pupils are learning. For youngsters it all helps make the language much more real than – for example – repetitive exercises in a language laboratory.

You can help your child – and stimulate their interest – by taking them abroad and by preparing and encouraging them to speak the language in shops or restaurants. If foreign travel is not possible, having foreign guests in your home can be a good stimulus to language learning. This can be done through exchange visits (many towns arrange these with their 'twins' in Europe) or by providing lodging to language students for the summer. Most language schools here try to place students with host families. Parents' own attitudes to learning foreign languages are also bound to influence children, so maybe now is the time to sign up for that Spanish evening class!

■ WHAT YOUR CHILD WILL STUDY

Over the years, the emphasis in foreign language teaching has shifted away from written work and repetitive oral exercises towards much greater emphasis on spoken language. The new curriculum continues this trend and pupils will be taught how to use their foreign language in a whole range of everyday activities and situations, such as going shopping or writing letters. They will also be expected to take part in more imaginative and creative activities during lessons.

So, throughout the first five years of secondary school, your children will learn about the specialist vocabulary of the following areas and their linguistic and cultural customs and conventions:

Everyday activities

This involves language used in everyday life at home and at school, covering activities such as shopping, eating out, sports and leisure.

Personal and social life

Pupils will earn to use the language needed when discussing their family and friends, special occasions such as holidays or family weddings, their attitudes towards religion and politics, and health.

The world around us

This covers topics such as homes, towns, regions of the country and the weather and natural surroundings.

Education, training, and work

Pupils will learn to use the language they will need to describe the subjects they are doing at school and the jobs they would like to do, and when dealing with business, industry and tourism.

Communications

This involves using the language needed when writing letters, using the telephone, reading newspapers, watching television and using computers.

The international world
This covers the language of foreign travel, school visits, international events and the different regions of the world.

Imagination and creativity
Pupils will use the language needed to discuss music, poetry, films, plays, painting and for talking about their hobbies and artistic interests.

In all of these settings, pupils will learn:

★ how to ask and answer questions.

★ how to improve pronunciation.

★ how to adapt their language to different audiences (for example to younger children).

★ how to write in different forms, such as diaries, letters, poems and stories.

★ how to read different types of text, such as postcards, newspapers or short stories.

★ how to learn by heart phrases or songs.

■ WHAT YOUR CHILD IS EXPECTED TO KNOW

Pupils will be graded on the ten-level scale on the basis of assessments made by their own teachers and on the more formal nationally-set tests. The current plan is to give equal weight to speaking, listening, reading and writing.

Although foreign languages are only part of the National Curriculum in secondary schools, there is still a full ten-point scale as with all other subjects. Clearly pupils are expected to move quickly through the lower levels, with the majority of pupils expected to have reached *Level Six* or higher by the age of 16.

At fourteen

After three years at secondary school, pupils take the first nationally-set tests in foreign languages at 14. Their score in this will be put together with assessments made by their own teacher during normal classwork to give an overall grade. Pupils of average ability should have reached around *Level Five* at 14. To achieve this, they should amongst other things be able to:

Listening
★ understand and respond to spoken language, for example in interviews with people talking about their jobs on television or radio.

★ understand the key points of a message, for example taking down the details of flight times and ticket prices over the telephone.

Speaking
★ keep up a simple conversation over more than one topic, such as school and hobbies.
★ make brief statements such as 'Last summer I went to Lowestoft with my family. We stayed at a holiday camp near the sea'.
★ put words in the correct order and use the correct forms of address, for example knowing when to use 'tu' or 'vous' in French.

Reading
★ understand relatively complex sentences (i.e. with one or more sub-clauses) in tourist brochures, newspaper articles, poems or songs.
★ make effective use of a simple English–foreign language dictionary, such as English–French or English–German.

Writing
★ produce a short piece of writing, for example describing a favourite person or place.
★ redraft written work correcting it and amending information.
★ generally use correct word order.

At sixteen
Most pupils will take a GCSE in their chosen language at 16, although there may be the option of taking a vocational qualification, such as a BTEC First Diploma which will be brought into line with National Curriculum requirements. By this age, the average pupil should have reached around *Level Six* or *Seven* on the National Curriculum ten-point scale. That is roughly equivalent to GCSE grades C to E. To achieve this, they should amongst other things be able to:

Listening
★ understand the main points of a television interview or an introductory passage on a sound cassette.
★ understand what is being said in a clear public announcement.

Speaking
★ use simple responses, questions and statements in unprompted conversation.

For example:
Q: 'What are you doing this weekend?'
A: 'I have nothing planned.'
Q: Would you like to come swimming with me?'
A: 'Yes. Let's go on Saturday morning.'
★ speak fairly fluently with correct intonation and – with simple sentences – making few mistakes.

Reading
★ understand selected writing from newspapers, magazines, advertisements etc.
★ select a library book appropriate to their own level.

Writing
★ write a simple dialogue for performance in drama or role-play.
★ write to a new penfriend, giving and asking for personal details.

To get a grade A at GCSE, pupils must reach *Level Nine or Ten* on the National Curriculum scale. To achieve this they should amongst other things be able to:

Listening
★ follow and understand television interviews or news items.
★ recognise the difference between types of spoken language, for example children's stories and television news reports.

Speaking
★ discuss a range of topics, backing up statements with opinions, in a group discussion.
★ speak with fluency, spontaneity, and good pronunciation.
★ make a reasoned presentation to others.

Reading
★ read a wide range of material from creative writing to official reports.
★ read independently and discuss responses to books.

Writing
★ write a letter to a newspaper about topical issues.
★ write a short speech or an article aimed at younger children.

10
TECHNOLOGY
■

WHAT DOES TECHNOLOGY INVOLVE?
WHAT WILL MY CHILD STUDY?
WHAT WILL MY CHILD BE EXPECTED TO KNOW?

■ WHAT DOES TECHNOLOGY INVOLVE?

Technology is a subject parents will not recognise from their own schooldays. It does have some things in common with the more familiar craft subjects and it also covers aspects of science. But it is a totally new subject. In essence, it is all about solving practical everyday problems which occur in the home, at work or in the community.

The aim is to teach youngsters to assess different methods for solving problems and then to carry them out. So as well as devising surveys or studies to assess the exact nature of a problem, they are also expected to select the appropriate methods and materials required. For example, deciding how to store books in a classroom or office involves decisions about which materials to use according to the money available, and questions of design, such as whether to use cupboards or shelves according to the need for ease of access or security.

It is different from, for example, woodwork or metalwork. In these subjects the emphasis was rather more on developing craft skills than on designing objects. Some say that the new broader subject fails to give pupils the same level of craft skills. This is almost certainly true, but it does prepare them to think about and design things for themselves, rather than following other people's designs.

The more familiar subjects embraced by technology include: art and design, woodwork, metalwork, business studies and the use of computers. The idea of bringing all these under one umbrella and making it compulsory is one of the most innovative aspects of the new curriculum. Technology is separate from science, but linked to it.

In secondary schools, it is likely to have its own separate place on the school timetable. In primary schools it will usually be approached through projects or themes, often overlapping with science. Clearly, in primary schools there will be a narrower range of equipment and materials, with rather more use of cardboard than teak!

Technology is not designed primarily as a vocational course, although it has clear value for most jobs which involve problem-solving, ingenuity and team-work. All aspects of technology are intended for boys and girls alike. Indeed, it will not be possible for boys to do only activities like construction or for girls to stick to design. Some single-sex schools, particularly boys-only schools, will have to broaden their range of teaching expertise and equipment in order to meet the full range of this subject. All children must take technology up to the age of 16, but it is not compulsory to take a GCSE in the subject.

There are five main areas of skills which technology is intended to encourage. Together they make up the process of identifying a need, making a design proposal, planning a system or making an item, evaluating the end product and using information technology.

Identifying needs and opportunities
Pupils learn how to find out about the needs and the potential for design and technology in a range of settings, such as the home, school, the community, industry and business.

Producing a design proposal
Pupils learn how to make design proposals to meet the needs they have identified. This includes deciding which materials to use, taking into account availability and cost, and exploring the possibilities and problems involved before producing a final detailed proposal.

Planning and making
The next stage covers working out plans to turn designs into reality, using a wide range of materials such as textiles, paint, clay, wood, metal or plastic.

Evaluating
Pupils learn to form their own views on the advantages and disadvantages of different designs and products made either by themselves or by others. This includes looking at things made in earlier times and other cultures.

Using information technology

Information technology is all about storing, processing and presenting information by electronic means. Pupils will learn how to make use of computers in their own work, for word-processing, spreadsheets, storing data, and to generate graphics or sounds. They will also learn how electronic devices are built into washing machines, automatic doors, tape recorders etc. to make them work according to pre-set programmes.

In primary schools information technology is increasingly important. The availability of computers is still very patchy, but overall the ratio is about one computer for every 40 children.

Information technology and other subjects

The use of computers comes into several other National Curriculum subjects. In English, for example, pupils are expected to use word processors to draft and re-draft their work. In mathematics, pupils are expected to handle data on a computer. In both cases, children are expected to use computers from as young as five.

■ WHAT YOUR CHILD WILL STUDY

From five to seven

Clearly, at this age your child will not be expected to build or design complicated objects. The very word 'technology' might at first seem odd in this context. But from the moment they start playing with building bricks, plasticine and card children are designing and constructing objects. Many toys include simple mechanical workings. So you can do much to help your child at home by encouraging them to make and build things. Give them a range of materials – card, paper, clay, wood, glue and so on – to make things with. There are lots of toys, too, which encourage designing and making things.

In the first years at school, they will be building on their own early experience of playing with objects. So they will learn by looking at objects that surround them in everyday life, for example how we use simple machines to make jobs easier.

The following are just some of the sorts of activities they will probably be involved in:

★ learning that a system in made up of related parts which are combined for a purpose as in, for example, a bicycle.

★ making models of simple structures, such as model houses.

★ using sources of energy to make things move, such as seeing how a

battery runs a toy or how a stretched elastic band can propel an object.
★ exploring a variety of materials to design and make things, e.g. cotton reels to build a tower or fabric and card to make a collage.
★ developing ideas by making sketches, talking and writing about them, and making models from materials such as card, wire or clay.
★ learning to use simple tools, such as scissors or a grater.
★ recognising that goods are designed, made and distributed.

For work on *information technology*, children will be taught to:
★ control everyday items, such as central heating thermostats and televisions.
★ organise and present ideas on a simple word processor package.
★ locate and retrieve information stored in a database.

From seven to eleven

As they move on to the juniors, children will be taught to look more critically at designs and man-made objects of all types. They will start to look at examples taken from beyond their normal everyday experience. Activities will include:
★ learning to develop ideas, organise and plan work within a group of pupils by, for example, making a nature area or producing a puppet theatre.
★ learning to identify the parts of a system and their function, for example the triangular frameworks in pylons.
★ learning to select appropriate materials, in terms of their cost, weight and availability.
★ developing appreciation of aesthetic qualities in natural and man-made objects, such as honeycombs or decorative tiles.
★ improving the way they communicate their ideas, for example by producing scripts and/or story-boards.
★ drawing plans for three-dimensional objects.
★ learning how to find out what customers want, for example by surveying attitudes to clothes or school meals.
★ appreciating that goods can be designed to be produced singly or in large quantities, and that this affects how much they cost.

For the older or more able pupils within the junior school, rather more sophisticated activities will include:
★ making a simple system and considering how to improve it e.g. a working model of a drawbridge.
★ using mechanisms to change one type of motion into another e.g. gears, pulleys and levers.

★ recognising the aesthetic qualities of natural and manufactured objects e.g. the grain in wood, the colour of bricks.

★ drawing and modelling using plans, elevations, sections, templates and perspectives.

★ learning how advertising is used to promote and sell goods.

★ learning that the cost of making something includes time, people, equipment and materials.

★ learning to reflect on how they went about a task and how they might do it differently next time.

In *information technology*, children should be taught to:

★ retrieve and amend text on a word processor.

★ know that information technology can be used to do things which can also be done in other ways, e.g. using a database rather than a card index.

★ assess their use of information technology and consider how it is used in the outside world, e.g. by comparing the way they have produced a class newspaper with real newspaper production.

From 11 to 14

In the early years at secondary school, younsters will be able to make use of a much wider range of equipment and tools. The tasks they attempt will be more open-ended. In other words, they must find answers and solutions for themselves. Some activities will probably take them out of the school itself.

So at this age pupils should be taught to:

★ sort a task into component parts and the order they must be done in, e.g. planning a meal course by course and its preparation.

★ assess systems to see how they can be improved, e.g. nearby road traffic layout.

★ test objects to see if they perform as intended, e.g. checking whether waterproof clothes really do keep out the rain.

★ select materials when making an object, taking into account cost and availability, e.g. making a musical instrument.

★ discover how aesthetic qualities influence consumers' choices, e.g. the shape or colour of food packaging.

★ investigate the effects of design and technological activity on the environment e.g. motorway construction.

At this level, for their use of *information technology*, pupils should be taught to:

★ use words, pictures, symbols and sounds to make a presentation, e.g. using a desk-top publishing package with graphs and charts and

using tape-recorders for accompanying commentary.
★ use graphics programmes for computer display.
★ select the appropriate software for a particular task.

From 14 to 16

At this age many – but not all – students will be working towards their GCSE. Visits and work outside school are encouraged at this stage, including work experience placements where students spend time in a factory, office or other workplace. Students may also undertake an extended design and technological task, involving between 15 and 30 hours' work.

Activities should include:
★ estimating the operating costs and efficiency of a system, for example when choosing between gas and electricity for central heating.
★ devising ways of reducing energy loss in the home, office or factory.
★ designing items for particular customers, for example a radio for teenagers.
★ using a computer to control a model lift, car park barrier or burglar alarm.
★ considering the social and environmental effects of a new motorway.
★ using modelling techniques to communicate design proposals.
★ developing, marketing, promoting and selling a product, such as a healthy snack food.

Pupils who are capable of reaching the higher levels in the National Curriculum might do the following activities:
★ evaluating market-research methods, for example to decide on the siting of a new supermarket.
★ learning how to dispose of waste in an environmentally safe way.
★ designing symbols and signs which make sense without language, for example for international travellers at an airport.
★ using computer-aided design to plan the layout of new kitchen.
★ developing proposals for a new company logo and letterhead.
★ designing a road bridge, using models to test for strength in high winds.
★ developing effective pricing, promotion and distribution e.g. by setting up a company to design and sell badges.

In *information technology*, pupils should be taught to:
★ select appropriate software e.g. choose between a word-

processing or a desk-top publishing package to develop a book for young readers.

★ design a computer-based system for recording information e.g. for recording pupils' preferences for school meals.

★ create databases for different purposes e.g. for a paint manufacturer to identify customers' preferences for colour and type of paint.

■ WHAT YOUR CHILD IS EXPECTED TO KNOW
At seven

The first National Curriculum testing is at seven. There are no compulsory national tests in technology. However there will be tests which teachers can use as part of their continuing assessment of children's progress against National Curriculum targets.

The average seven-year-old is expected to be at about *Level Two* on the National Curriculum scale. To achieve that they must be able to show that, amongst other things, they are able to:

★ ask questions to identify the needs and opportunities for design and technology activity, e.g. finding out how the school cook chooses the menus for school dinners.

★ use pictures, drawings, models and their own words to develop designs, e.g. design a scarecrow and say how it will scare birds.

★ use simple tools and materials for making things, e.g. tools for cutting and shaping clay.

★ make judgements on the usefulness and appearance of different designs and products, e.g. evaluating different types of cutlery from baby spoons to chopsticks.

In *information technology* they should be able to do the following when using simple computers in the classroom:

★ understand and use pictures, words, and symbols displayed on a computer screen, e.g. construct a simple story using pictures or words in a sequence.

★ write and then store words on a computer.

At eleven

The second round of testing takes place at the end of primary school, by which time most children will be 11. It is not yet clear whether there will be national written tests in technology. There will, though, be assessments made by class teachers according to National Curriculum guidelines. By this stage the average pupil is expected to have reached around *Level Four* on the National Curriculum scale.

132

A PARENTS' GUIDE TO THE NEW CURRICULUM

Amongst other things, they should be able to show they can do the following in their design and technology:

★ identify the opportunities and demand for design and technology in a specific area, e.g. devise a questionnaire for classmates to find out what they like and dislike about the playground and then design improvements, taking into account the cost of any changes.

★ know that in the past people have overcome problems by using technology in different ways, e.g. different approaches to irrigation in different countries.

★ draft a design, discuss improvements and produce a final model and plan, e.g. for a lighthouse.

★ work with others to plan and carry out a task, using appropriate materials, e.g. allocating tasks to gather and write up information for a school newspaper and working out how to produce it.

★ understand how new products and technologies can change social and economic life, e.g. how convenience foods have changed lifestyles.

In *information technology*, the average 11-year-old should be able to:

★ use a computer to organise and present work, e.g. a class newsletter.

★ add to and correct information in a database, e.g. store personal information (name, age, height etc.), check it is correct, and use it to find children with the same characteristics.

At fourteen

Towards the end of the third year in secondary school, when most pupils are 14, pupils will take national written tests in technology. Their work will also be assessed by their own teachers on the basis of normal class work. Pupils will be graded according to the ten levels of the National Curriculum. At 14, the average pupil should be at around *Level Five* or *Six* on the National Curriculum scale. To achieve this, some of the things they should be able to do include:

★ use different sources of information to design ways of improving the way we do things, e.g. using questionnaires and books to assess eating habits and to devise ways to encourage healthier eating.

★ understand how new technologies create new demands, e.g. the the microwave cooker and the new products in supermarkets.

★ draft, improve and present design ideas in more detail, including which materials and tools are to be used.

★ use knowledge of the different qualities of materials to identify the most suitable for a particular design.

★ evaluate the design of a product, for example the visual appearance, durability, comfort and cost of an item of clothing.

In *information technology*, to reach Level Five or Six pupils should be able to:

★ understand that a computer can control devices by a series of commands, e.g. how automatic doors or alarm systems work.

★ use more sophisticated forms of word-processing, e.g. using desktop publishing to integrate words and images in a report.

At sixteen

Pupils reach the end of the National Curriculum at the age of 16 when testing for most is the GCSE. The student of average ability is expected to reach *Level Six* or *Seven* on the National Curriculum ten-point scale. Level Six is broadly equivalent to the current GCSE grade D or E, and Level Seven is roughly the same as a grade C or D.

The reach Level Six/Seven, pupils should amongst other things be able to do the following:

★ do a feasibility study on new systems, e.g. of recycling household waste, looking at prices, costs, benefits etc.

★ show how to evaluate designs through tests, experiments or pilot models.

★ show competency in the skilled use of materials and tools, e.g. measuring and marking out materials accurately.

★ understand the wider effects of new technologies on societies past and present, e.g. the impact of mass-produced plastic goods on developing countries.

In *information technology*, the average 16-year-old should be able to:

★ select and use the most suitable software for specific purposes, e.g. to produce a presentation to an adult audience.

★ use information technology to interpret data transmitted by a weather satellite.

To reach *Level Nine* (GCSE grade A) or *Ten* (A+), pupils should amongst other things be able to do the following:

★ use videos, models, diagrams and cost data to justify a project, such as the extension of the school library.

★ create a design for a project and make a presentation on it, including a comprehensive folio of drawings, sketches, and models.

★ use computer-aided designs and high quality graphics to produce a new corporate image for a business.

★ show they can evaluate their own work and the work of others.

11
HISTORY

■

WHAT DOES HISTORY INVOLVE?

WHAT WILL MY CHILD STUDY?

WHAT WILL MY CHILD BE EXPECTED TO KNOW?

■ WHAT DOES HISTORY INVOLVE?

History is a subject that has tended to lose its individual identity in recent years. In primary schools, and in the early years of secondary school, it had become common for history to be taught as part of social studies or humanities. Sometimes it was barely taught at all in primary schools, especially in the infants. The National Curriculum makes it compulsory throughout primary school, although it will often be covered through topic work which combines other subjects with history. In secondary schools – where it is compulsory up to 14 – it will in future be taught mostly as a separate subject. Here too the new curriculum should mean more pupils studying history.

CHOICES FOR 14-YEAR-OLDS

Pupils can choose between:

● continuing with history *and* geography (leading to two GCSE awards).

● choosing *either* history *or* geography (one GCSE).

● taking a *combined* history/geography course which is narrower than the two subjects taken separately (one GCSE).

● taking full history and a short course in geography or vice versa (see also page 146).

After 14, pupils have a choice between continuing with history, dropping it in favour of geography or taking shorter, combined courses in both history and geography. They can also choose to take a full course in history and a short course in geography or vice versa.

Pupils will also be able to combine a short course in history with another subject, provided they also study at least a short course in geography.

History has been the most controversial subject in the National Curriculum. This was perhaps inevitable as history deals with political issues. Teachers are, of course, required by law to give a balanced presentation of opposing views when teaching controversial issues. However many people have felt uncomfortable with the idea of the government of the day deciding what should be taught in school history.

In the past, individual schools and teachers had great freedom in their choice of the periods of history they taught. Now the National Curriculum aims to ensure comprehensive coverage of history for all. It should no longer be possible to leave school without having learnt at least something about the Roman Empire or Victorian Britain.

There is still some choice over periods or topics, but only within carefully designed limits. All pupils must study British, European and some world history. They should also have the chance to study local history throughout primary and secondary school. This can be history of their home area – their school, village or town – or of the wider region.

British history takes the central role but pupils are expected to relate our own history to what went on in the wider world. The new curriculum follows a broad chronological sweep, but without plodding slavishly from the Ancient Greeks in the infant school to Modern Britain for GCSE pupils. There is some jumping ahead – and some back-tracking – along the way.

WHO STUDIES WHAT?

Infants (5–7)
A broad introduction to the past, through their own family and local area, with glimpses of the more distant past through story, myth, custom and legend.

Juniors (7–11)
Ancient Greece and the Roman Empire to either Victorian or Modern Britain.

Secondary (11–14)
Roman Empire to the Second World War.

Secondary (14–16)
Mainly twentieth century.

National Curriculum history sets out the countries and periods to be studied and the historical skills that pupils should develop. It encourages several different approaches to the past, including political, economic, social and cultural history. Pupils are also taught to use a range of historical sources, such as:
★ documents and books.
★ man-made objects.
★ pictures and photographs.
★ music.
★ buildings and sites.

When does history end?
There has been considerable argument over the question 'when does history end?'. In recent years, the answer from most schools would have been 'yesterday'. The GCSE included contemporary history on the basis that it helped youngsters to understand the modern world. But the government decided that secondary school history should not include current affairs and imposed a cut-off point for history in the 1960s. So, for example, National Curriculum studies of Russia and the USSR end with the fall of Krushchev in 1964 and events in the USA end with the assassination of President Kennedy in 1963. It seems likely that this odd state of affairs will be reviewed soon.

Primary school pupils can however bring their study of history right up to the present day.

1066 and all that?
There has also been debate over how history should be taught. This has been oversimplified as a battle between those who think history is about learning facts against those who believe it is all about teaching youngsters to develop skills of historical inquiry and analysis. The latter skills-based approach has grown in popularity with teachers, particularly since the introduction of the GCSE.

This change was partly a response to the idea of history as rote-learning of facts, such as the dates of battles. This '1066 and all that' approach, it was argued, left youngsters with a good knowledge of dates but little understanding of the events they marked. However, the National Curriculum has seen some ground being won back by those who believe historical content is more important than skills. This camp – which had the support of senior Conservatives – argued that to develop skills before children had a good grasp of the facts was putting the cart before the horse.

The battle-lines were never that clearly defined. Those who favour the skills approach have never argued that children should not learn facts. Equally those who want more emphasis on factual content do not advocate a return to history as pure rote-learning. The experts who devised the National Curriculum history course said that they regarded the debate as sterile. They have managed to steer something of a middle way through what continue to be choppy waters.

■ WHAT YOUR CHILD WILL STUDY
From five to seven
In the infants, history will usually be taught through topics designed to give children an awareness of the past and an understanding of how it differs from the present. The starting point is usually children's own families and experiences, such as visits to museums or historic sites. They will also learn about the past through pictures, photographs and stories set in the past, including myths and legends from various cultures.

Topics will introduce them to everyday life in the past, looking at the clothes we used to wear and the houses we lived in. Other historical themes might include diet, shops, transport and different types of entertainment. Parents can help by discussing with their children how things have changed since they or their own parents were children. By relating events to when grandma was a girl – or when you were young yourself – you can begin to give children a sense of the time-scale of history.

By the second year in the infant school, children might focus on the past two generations of their own family. The more distant past will be explored through stories about fictional characters or real people. They will also be introduced to the past through events that have been commemorated by many generations, such as Guy Fawkes night or the Olympic Games. Topics may well include 'My School', 'Famous People', or 'Toys and Games'.

From seven to eleven
In the juniors, history begins to take on a more traditional look, focusing on particular peoples and periods. During their time in the juniors, pupils must learn about:
★ Invaders and settlers: Romans, Anglo-Saxons, and Vikings in Britain.

★ Tudor and Stuart times.
★ Victorian Britain and/or Britain since 1930.
★ Ancient Greece.
★ Exploration and encounters 1450 to 1550.
   Schools can decide for themselves in what order they will teach these periods. But the new curriculum does say what must be taught within each period.

Invaders and Settlers in Britain
● *Romans*
The Roman conquest and settlement of Britain.
Boudicca's attempt to resist the Romans.
Britain in the Roman Empire and the departure of the Romans.
● *Anglo-Saxons*
Anglo-Saxon invasions and settlements, including the rule of King Alfred.
The conversion of Britain by Roman and Celtic Christians.
● *Vikings*
Viking raids and settlement.
The wider Viking world.

Tudor and Stuart times
The Tudor and Stuart monarchs.
Major events, including the Armada, Civil War, Restoration, Great Plague and the Great Fire of London.
Important people, including Newton, Shakespeare, Drake and Raleigh.

Victorian Britain
Steam-power, industry and child labour.
The railways.
The growth of towns.
The start of public health and education.
Religion and science.
How Victorian families lived.

Britain since 1930
The impact of the Second World War.
Changes in the role of men and women.
Inventions and discoveries.
Popular culture, including the radio, cinema and television.

Ancient Greece
Athens and Sparta.
Citizens and slaves.
Greek gods, myths and legends.
The Persian Wars.
Politics, sport and the arts.

Exploration and encounters 1450 to 1550
Maps of the world in the late fifteenth century.
The search for a route to the Spice Islands, including the voyages of
  Columbus.
Montezuma and the Aztec Empire.
The Spanish conquest of the Aztec Empire.
The growth of trade between the Old and the New World.

As well as these specific periods, junior school pupils must do
some local history. This can relate to one of the periods above, such
as Victorian Britain. They must also look at history over a long period
of time through the study of one specific theme, such as 'Ships
and seafarers', 'Food and farming' or 'Land Transport'. Finally
they must study one non-European society, for example, Ancient
Egypt.

From 11 to 14
Over the first three years in secondary school your child must be
taught about the following peoples and periods:
★ The Roman Empire.
★ Medieval Britain 1066 to 1500.
★ The making of the United Kingdom 1500 to 1750.
★ Expansion, trade and industry: Britain 1750 to 1900.
★ The Second World War.

Once again, the required content of each of these periods is
clearly set down, as follows:

The Roman Empire
The formation of the Empire and the reign of Augustus.
The expansion of the Empire.
Roman technology, including roads and water systems.
The Roman way of life.
The development of Christianity.
Roman art, architecture, and literature.
The barbarian invasions and the sack of Rome.

Medieval realms: Britain 1066 to 1500
Christendom and the British Isles' place in Europe.
The Norman Conquest and the Battle of Hastings.
English medieval monarchy and the Church, barons and people.
Magna Carta and the Peasants' Revolt.
The origins of Parliament.
Relations between England, Ireland, Scotland and Wales.
Health and disease, including the Black Death.

The making of the United Kingdom: 1500 to 1750
The formation of the United Kingdom, including the Acts of Union
  and the Treaty of 1707.
The Crown, Parliament and the people in the Civil War and Inter-
  regnum and the Glorious Revolution.
The scientific revolution in the seventeenth century.
Relations between Roman Catholics, Anglicans and Nonconformists.

Expansion, trade and industry: Britain 1750 to 1900
Changes in agriculture, industry and transport.
The impact of industrialisation on families and communities.
The expansion of the Empire.
Parliament and politics.
Popular protest and the extension of the franchise, including the
  Great Reform Act of 1832.

The Second World War
The legacy of the First World War.
Co-operation and conflict in the 1930s.
Wartime leaders, including Hitler, Churchill, Stalin and Roosevelt.
Britain in wartime.
The Holocaust.
The atomic bombs on Hiroshima and Nagasaki.
The impact of the war across the world.
The redrawing of national boundaries.
    As well as these periods, pupils must undertake a number of
more detailed studies, including one on Britain, one on Europe and
one on a non-European society. Some suggested topics include:

Britain
Castles and cathedrals 1066 to 1500.
Britain and the American Revolution.

The impact of the Industrial Revolution on a local area.
Britain and the Great War 1914–1918.

Europe
The Crusades.
The Italian Renaissance.
The French Revolution.
German and Italian unification.

World
Islamic civilisations.
Imperial China.
India from the Mughal Empire to the coming of the British.
Indigenous peoples of North America.

From 14 to 16
The last part of the history curriculum rounds off the broad sweep of
history by concentrating on events in the twentieth century up to the
1960s. Pupils will look at history from political, economic, social,
religious and cultural angles.

At 14 – as they set out on their GCSE courses – pupils may
choose to do either the full history course or a short course which
they can combine with a similarly reduced course in geography or
other subjects such as a language, as long as they also do at least a
short course in geography. Those opting for the short course must
study twentieth-century Britain, Europe and the wider world. Their
studies will follow three main themes:

The development of British democracy 1900–1960s
★ the extension of the parliamentary franchise in 1918, 1928 and
1969.
★ the reasons for change in the political party system.
★ differences between British democracy and other systems.
★ the United Kingdom and the Irish Free State/Eire.
★ the development of the welfare state.

International conflict and co-operation 1945–1960s
★ superpower relations since the Second World War.
★ the break up of the European empires.
★ the United Nations and international co-operation.
★ political and economic co-operation in Europe 1945 to 1970.

Economic, social and cultural change in the twentieth century
This covers major world developments with particular reference to
Britain, including:
★ changing economies and their effect on work, environment and
everyday life.
★ the world impact of cultural, ethnic and religious differences.
★ the growth of mass communications and popular culture.
★ population changes.
    Pupils who have chosen to take the full history course, leading to
a single-subject GCSE award in history, must study all the above as
well as the following:

★ *an important theme in British history starting at least before 1500 and
continuing to the present day*
This is intended to build on earlier work on pre-twentieth century
history. Typical themes might be: Parliament; Public health;
Education; Agriculture; Work; Migration; Popular culture.

★ *a country or region other than Britain in the twentieth century*
This topic can be chosen from the following:
Russia and the USSR from the 1905 Revolution to the downfall of
    Krushchev.
The USA from entry to the First World War to the assassination of
    President Kennedy.
The Indian sub-continent from the First World War to the death of
    Nehru.
Africa south of the Sahara from the Boer War to the independence of
    Kenya.
The Middle East from the First World War to the Six-Day War.
Latin America from the Mexican Revolution to the Cuba Crisis.
Japan from the Russo-Japanese War to becoming a major economic
    power.
China from the Chinese Revolution to the Cultural Revolution.

■ WHAT YOUR CHILD IS EXPECTED TO KNOW
The experts who devised the National Curriculum had a particular
problem when it came to deciding how to test pupils' knowledge of
history. For example, they have not set out which dates must be
learnt. This is because one date is as easy or difficult to remember as
another and therefore it is impossible to grade them according to the

different levels of the National Curriculum. So assessments will be made on the basis of pupils' overall grasp of history and the skills needed to understand and interpret it. However, they will have to demonstrate they know the key historical facts and dates of the periods outlined above and must always relate their skills to the content of the periods they have studied.

At seven

As children approach the end of the infants school, they will be assessed against the ten-point scale of the National Curriculum. There is no compulsory, written test for history, as there is in English, mathematics and science. Instead the assessment will be made by pupil's own teachers on the basis of their normal classwork, although teachers may choose to use written tests as well if they wish.

The average seven-year-old is expected to have reached *Level Two*. To achieve this they must show they know the historical content of the periods they have been studying and – amongst other things – should be able to:

★ put familiar objects (such as family photographs) in chronological order.

★ explain reasons for what happened in the past, such as why the Britons fought against the Romans.

★ show they recognise the difference between the past and present, for example by talking about how life is different today from in the Victorian period.

★ recognise that two people can give different accounts of the same events.

★ recognise that stories from the past and old items (such as museum exhibits) help us to understand the past.

Children who are progressing faster than average may reach *Level Three* if they are able to:

★ give reasons for important historical events, such as why railways became more important than canals as a form of transport in the nineteenth century.

★ understand differences between times in the past, for example the difference between an ancient Greek temple and a medieval cathedral.

★ know the difference between a fact and a point of view.

★ make deductions from historical sources, such as recognising social class from the clothes of Victorian people.

At eleven

At the end of primary school children are assessed for the second time against the National Curriculum ten-point scale. The first national tests for this age do not begin until 1994, and it is not yet clear whether there will be compulsory written tests in history. However, pupils will be assessed against the ten-level scale by their own teacher.

The average 11-year-old should be at around *Level Four*. To achieve this, they must show they know the content of the period they have been studying and – amongst other things – be able to:

★ recognise that over time some things have changed quickly while others have changed very little.

★ show they recognise that most events have more than one explanation and effect.

★ describe different features of one historical period, such as a range of aspects of life in Tudor Britain.

★ understand that inadequate or unreliable evidence may lead to incomplete pictures of the past.

★ put together information on one period drawn from several sources, for example from old newspapers, photographs and maps.

At fourteen

After three years at secondary school, pupils will take national, written tests in history, although these will probably not be introduced before 1995. Pupils will also be assessed by their own teachers on the basis of classwork and will be graded according to the ten-level scale of the National Curriculum.

The average 14-year-old is expected to be somewhere between *Level Five and Six*. They should amongst other things be able to:

★ recognise that historical change can be local or national and gradual or quick.

★ identify different types of causes and effects, for example social or political and short-term or long-term.

★ recognise that some causes and consequences of major events are more important than others.

★ give an account of different views of a major event or situation, for example the range of reactions to the coming of the railways in Victorian Britain.

★ demonstrate that historical interpretations depend on the selection of sources.

★ compare the usefulness of different historical sources.

At sixteen

At 16 the formal assessment of most pupils' final position on the ten-point scale of the National Curriculum comes in the shape of the GCSE. Pupils of average ability are expected to be around *Level Six or Level Seven*. This is equivalent in the old GCSE terms of a grade C to E. So a pupil scoring half way between level six and seven would be of the same standard as a grade D. The new ten-point scale replaces the A to G grades from 1994 onwards.

To achieve *Level Six* or *Seven*, pupils should be able to:

★ show an understanding that 'change' and 'progress' are not the same (for example, show an understanding of how public health in the early nineteenth century improved in some ways (medical progress) but deteriorated in others (worsening social conditions).

★ understand that change is not uniform and affects different social classes and different regions in varying ways.

★ show how the many different causes of historical change are interlinked (for example, the connections between technological innovation and economic growth in improving living standards).

★ show how opinions and political views relate to circumstances (for example, how economic hardship led the French people to support the Revolution of 1789).

★ recognise that different accounts of events have varying strengths and weaknesses as interpretations of what happened.

★ make informed judgements about the validity of historical sources (for example, recognising that the reliability of newspapers can be affected by the views of the writer or the owner of the publication).

Pupils who reach *Level Nine* or *Ten* – the equivalent of an A grade at GCSE – should be able to:

★ show how causes, motives and consequences may be related (for example, giving an account of the Second World War, making connections between the consequences of the First World War, the motives of Hitler, and the causes and consequences of the contemporary political mood of the German people).

★ explain why individuals do not necessarily share the views of their social class or the rest of society (for example, the suffragettes).

★ explain why different groups interpret history in different ways (for example, the different views of the significance of Lenin).

★ show an understanding of the difficulties involved in trying to make history as objective as possible.

★ recognise that the usefulness of a source depends on the questions asked of it.

12
GEOGRAPHY

■

WHAT DOES GEOGRAPHY INVOLVE?

WHAT WILL MY CHILD STUDY?

WHAT WILL MY CHILD BE EXPECTED TO KNOW?

■ WHAT DOES GEOGRAPHY INVOLVE?

Geography is compulsory in the new curriculum for all children from five to 14. After that, pupils working towards their GCSEs at 16 have various options. Short courses alone do not lead to a GCSE, but when combined with other subjects may lead either to a GCSE or an equivalent vocational qualification.

CHOICES FOR 14-YEAR-OLDS
Pupils can choose between:
- continuing with full courses in geography **and** history (leading to two GCSE awards).
- choosing either geography **or** history (one GCSE).
- taking full geography **and** a short course in history or vice versa.
- taking short courses in **both** subjects, combined either with each other or with other subjects.

Geography does not fit neatly into the category of either science or arts. It has long been lumped together with history and described as 'the humanities' or taught under the broad heading of environmental studies. In secondary schools the National Curriculum should give it new life as a separate subject. Before the National Curriculum a very large proportion of pupils abandoned geography at 14. Frequent surveys have shown that adults in Britain are not very good at locating cities in their own country never mind elsewhere in the world.

Geography is all about the study of places and the way they have been shaped by either human or physical activity. It is also about the people who live in these places. In other words, it is about making sense of the world about us from the rocks beneath our feet to the weather in the atmosphere around us. The key questions are 'where?', 'what?', 'how?' and 'why?'. The other basic question – 'when?' – applies more to history, but also has its place in geography.

The government changed the original plans of its advisers and insisted on greater emphasis on factual knowledge – such as the names and locations of cities, rivers and mountains – and rather less on geographical skills and political and economic issues. However, this does not mean a return to the old rote-learning approach with pupils memorising the names of the capes and bays of the world.

In the past, teachers have had considerable freedom over which parts of the world they taught. Now there are much tighter guidelines. As with history, this should ensure your child covers the most important aspects of the subject. The National Curriculum starts with children's own local area and works outwards, to the local region, the United Kingdom, Europe and the world. Rather like the classic diary address – you know the sort of thing 'Joe Bloggs, 122 Notley Road, Braintree, Essex, England, the UK, Europe, the World, the Universe' – the new curriculum tries to establish the relationships between geography on different scales.

Geography in the National Curriculum falls into five main areas:

Geographical skills
This covers the main skills needed for the study of geography, principally the use of maps and fieldwork techniques, such as measuring and recording weather observations.

Knowledge and understanding of places
From the age of five onwards, pupils must study their local area, a different locality elsewhere in the UK, and another country. For younger children, the local area may simply cover the immediate vicinity of their school or home. For older children it will be their local region.

Physical geography
This covers the nature of the earth's surface and the ways in which it changes. This includes: weather and climate; rivers, seas, and oceans; landforms; and animals, plants and soil.

Human geography
This covers how the land is used, where people live and how they work. It includes: population; settlements; communications and transport; and economic activities.

Environmental geography
This is the 'green' bit of the geography curriculum. Pupils are expected to develop an 'informed concern' about people's effect on the natural environment. This includes pollution, the use and misuse of resources and ways of protecting environments. Pupils are expected to understand that these issues involve conflicting pressures and are seen differently by different cultures.

How can parents help?
The nature of geography in the primary school makes it an excellent subject for parents to get involved in. Most of the geography your child will do at school will be based on developing simple skills and observing the local environment. So you can help your child by pointing out and discussing features of your own village, town or district. Try to have large-scale maps (the National Curriculum makes much use of Ordnance Survey 1:50,000 maps), a globe and an atlas at home. Use and discuss them with your children. Show them where Grandma lives and the road you take to drive there. You might also like to introduce a tape measure or compass into games you play with your child. You could try collecting rainfall in jam-jars and try to give explanations for different types of weather. Children at this age are usually full of questions about what they can see around them. Encourage this and – as far as you can – try to give them answers.

With older children, you can complement their work on foreign countries by collecting postcards, showing them your old holiday photographs and buying and discussing food from abroad (exotic fruit or Indian take-aways!) Any commonplace items which you or friends can bring back from abroad can also add a lot to your child's interest in another country. Bus tickets, newspapers, food wrappings, tourist maps and brochures all add a human feel to the study of a distant country. Your child's school may also welcome offers of such items.

■ WHAT YOUR CHILD WILL STUDY
From five to seven
In the infants, geography is likely to be taught through topic work,

although some schools may prefer to teach it as a separate subject. A typical topic for this age group would be 'Homes'. This could involve children looking at different types of homes in their area and in other parts of the world. They might then look at why different weather conditions have led to different types of homes. Most geography for this age group will be based on children's own interests and experience.

Other typical school topics for this age group include:

★ Where I live.
★ How I get to school.
★ People who help us.
★ The seasons.
★ Growing things.
★ Shops and shopping.

In developing *geographical skills*, children will be introduced to maps and globes, learning how to recognise land and sea. They will also learn how to follow a route on, for example, a map of the local area. Using pictures they will start to differentiate between different geographical forms, such as rivers, hills, lakes, mountains. They will also learn how to describe and record the weather.

More able pupils towards the end of this age group will learn how to use the eight points of the compass and how to use co-ordinates to find features on maps. They should also be learning how to make a map of a short route, such as from their home to school.

For children of this age *knowledge of places* will be based mainly on selected localities. This will include the area in the vicinity of the school and small, distinctive areas elsewhere. They will be taught to name and locate their local area in its wider context. For example, they will be taught that Latchmere Infants School is in Kingston-upon-Thames, which is in Surrey, which in turn is in England, which is a part of the United Kingdom.

In looking at different localities, they will be taught how to identify familiar features – such as parks or churches – and to look at where people go to work or to enjoy themselves. By the end of the infants, the more able pupils should be taught how to use correct geographical terms, to explain – for example – why shops are sited in particular places and to recognise England, Scotland, Wales and Northern Ireland on a map of the United Kingdom.

In finding out about *physical geography*, children will be taught about soil, water and rocks and where they are found in different parts of the landscape, such as rivers, fields and mountains. They will also be taught about the effects of the weather and the changing seasons on their surroundings. So be prepared for those devastatingly obvious but hard-to-answer questions from your five or six-year-old about what causes the wind or why it only snows in winter!

In *human geography* they might learn how some homes are parts of villages while others are in towns or cities. They will be finding out why communities vary in size and how they are supported by people involved in different types of work. They will also be looking at different types of job and transport.

In *environmental geography*, children will be taught where common materials come from and how they are extracted (for example, how coal is mined). They will also be taught how to look at the ways activities have changed the environment and to look at ways they could improve their own surroundings.

From seven to eleven

In the juniors, children will be taught *geographical skills* involving the use of tape measures, compasses and thermometers. They should be familiar with the points of the compass and be able to use four-figure co-ordinates to find features on a map. They will also be shown how to find information in an atlas.

More able pupils towards the top of the junior school should be taught to recognise conventional map symbols on Ordnance Survey maps and to know how to use longitude and latitude to find places on maps.

Extending their *knowledge of places*, junior school children will be taught about:

★ their local area.
★ a different locality within the UK.
★ a locality in a developing country.
★ a locality in a European Community country outside the UK.

Physical geography will include earthquakes and volcanoes, rivers, channels, and tributaries. Erosion caused by rivers, waves, wind, and glaciers is also covered, as are weather conditions, with pupils learning about polar, temperate, and tropical regions.

For their *human geography*, children of this age will be taught about the different ways land is used, for example, for farming, quarrying, or building. They will begin to learn why population changes occur and the reasons why different forms of transport develop in different areas.

Finally, in *environmental geography* your child will learn about mining and its effect on the environment, about fresh water sources and ways in which damaged environments can be restored. Older pupils may be starting to learn about the differences between renewable and non-renewable resources.

From 11 to 14

In secondary school, your child is most likely to be taught geography as a separate subject. Some schools may continue the practice of teaching it alongside history, but the new curriculum lends itself to the separation of humanities back into single subjects.

Your child will by this stage be taught to develop more sophisticated *geographical skills* than they encountered in junior school. So, they will learn how to:

★ measure and record weather, using rain gauges and maximum/ minimum thermometers.

★ read grid-references and symbols on Ordnance Survey maps.

★ use a map and compass to follow a route.

In the early years at secondary school, pupils will develop their *knowledge of places* by studying their local area and the wider area. They should study:

★ the local area.

★ the region they live in.

★ one European Community country outside the UK, selected from France, Germany, Italy or Spain.

★ one economically developing country (from a list including Bangladesh, Brazil, China, Egypt, Ghana, India, Kenya, Nigeria, Pakistan or Venezuela).

★ the USA, Japan, and USSR.

The *physical geography* to be covered includes:

★ earthquakes and volcanoes and their global distribution.

★ the landforms found in river-valleys and on sea-coasts.

★ the patterns of weather over Britain and the world.

★ types of vegetation such as savannah grassland or tropical desert.

In *human geography*, pupils will be taught about population patterns, transport facilities, and the layout of villages and towns. They will look at different types of land-use in farming, manufacturing and retail industry.

In *environmental geography*, pupils will learn about the differences between manufactured goods and natural resources and will study the effect on the environment of at least two energy sources such as coal or nuclear energy.

From 14 to 16

From the age of 14 it is possible for your child to drop geography (providing they continue with history) or to follow a reduced geography course combined with another subject. The short course covers all five areas of the full course, but in less detail in each case. Pupils taking this course must still study both a European Community Country and a developing country, but they do not cover the USA, USSR and Japan. The following details assume your child is following the full geography course, leading to the GCSE.

To develop their *geographical skills*, pupils should amongst other things be taught to:

★ develop their map-reading, weather-measuring and use of atlases to a greater degree of precision.

★ use satellite images to identify patterns in physical and human geography.

★ measure and draw, to scale, local geographical features.

★ compare maps using different projections.

In developing their *knowledge of places* pupils will learn about the more general geography of whole countries and do a more detailed study of selected localties within those countries. They must be taught about:

★ their home region.

★ one European Community country chosen from France, Germany, Italy or Spain.

★ one theme (agriculture/tourism/population movement) across the European Community as a whole.

★ one economically developing country from Asia, Africa or South America.

★ a comparative study of the USA, Japan and USSR as well as a more detailed study of one of these three.

★ the broad pattern of international trade, with particular attention to the importance of Japan, in its relatively new role as a world economic power.

In *physical geography*, pupils will learn in more detail about weather and climate, volcanoes and earthquakes, and rivers and river basins. They will also begin more specialised study of:

★ landforms associated with highland glaciation or limestone features.

★ the influence of anticyclones and depressions on British weather.

★ the effects of weathering and erosion.

★ the pattern of ocean currents.

In *human geography*, pupils will be taught about
★ population movement.
★ different types of transport networks.
★ the reasons for differing layouts of towns and villages.
★ different types of land-use.
★ how to analyse why economic activities develop in some regions or countries and not others.

Environmental geography will involve, amongst other things, learning about:
★ how water supplies are polluted and how to solve pollution problems.
★ the effects on the environment of at least two energy sources (for example, coal and nuclear power).
★ ways of restoring damaged environments.
★ the causes and effects of global environmental change.

■ WHAT YOUR CHILD IS EXPECTED TO KNOW
At seven
At the end of the infants, there are no compulsory national tests in geography as there are in English, mathematics and science. However, geography tests for seven-year-olds are being devised and schools can use them if they wish. In the main, your child's level will be determined by the teacher's own assessment of pupil's work. They will award grades according to the National Curriculum ten-point scale.

The average seven-year-old should be at *Level Two*. To achieve that, some of the things they should know or be able to do include:
★ pick out features such as rivers, woods, roads from photographs.
★ discuss simple maps using terms such as slope, river, and hill.
★ identify England, Scotland, Wales and Northern Ireland on a map.
★ describe different types of farming, plants, weather and transport.
★ recognise different forms of water such as rain, clouds, rivers, frost and snow.
★ describe how we get basics like coal, wheat or fish from mining, farming and fishing.
★ know about ways in which people have changed the environment, through farming, building and pollution.

More able children who have reached *Level Three* on the National Curriculum scale should be capable of:

★ using simple grid references to locate features on a map.

★ locating major cities (London, Edinburgh, Cardiff, Belfast and Dublin), rivers (Thames, Trent, Severn) and areas (Lake District, Grampian Mountains, Pennines) on a map of the UK.

★ locating the continents and some important countries (USA, USSR, Australia, India and China) on world maps.

★ identifying, from maps and photographs, features such as ports, harbours, factories and market squares.

At eleven

At the end of the juniors – when the second formal assessment occurs – children of average ability should be at *Level Four* on the National Curriculum scale. To achieve this they should, amongst other things, be able to:

★ locate on a map of the UK:

Southampton, Bristol, Cardiff, London, Birmingham, Liverpool, Manchester, Leeds, Newcastle-Upon-Tyne, Glasgow, Edinburgh, Belfast, and Dublin.

The North-West Highlands, Grampians, Southern Uplands, Pennines, Lake District and Snowdonia.

★ locate on a map of Europe:

France, Germany, Italy, and Spain.

Berlin, Rome, Paris, and Madrid.

The Rhine; the Alps; the North Sea and the Mediterranean.

★ use four-figure co-ordinates to locate features on a map.

★ identify the parts of a river system, including source, channel, tributaries.

★ identify the main sources of fresh water (rivers, lakes and underground sources) and describe how it can be stored and supplied to users.

Eleven-year-olds of above average ability may have reached *Level Five* of the National Curriculum if they are capable of:

★ using six-figure grid references to find features on a map.

★ locating a wider range of major European cities.

★ locating capital cities elsewhere in the world.

★ explaining the causes and effects of river floods.

★ distinguishing between renewable and non-renewable resources.

At fourteen

Towards the end of the third year in secondary school, when most youngsters will be 14, they will take nationally-set, written tests in geography. They will also be assessed by their own teachers. Pupils of average ability should have reached around *Level Five* or *Six* of the National Curriculum. To achieve this they should, amongst other things, be able to:

★ locate on a map of Europe:

France, Spain, Italy, Germany, Portugal, Greece, Belgium, Luxembourg, the Netherlands, and Denmark.

Athens, Rome, Madrid, Paris, Brussels, Berlin, Copenhagen, Amsterdam.

The Danube, and the Rhine.

★ locate on a map of the world:

Canada, the USA, Mexico, Peru, Argentina, Venezuela, Brazil, Ghana, Nigeria, South Africa, Kenya, Egypt, Saudi Arabia, Israel, the USSR, Pakistan, India, Bangladesh, China, Japan, Indonesia, Australia, and New Zealand.

The Rockies, Great Lakes, Panama Canal, Andes, Sahara, Suez Canal, Himalayas.

Major rivers, including the Mississippi, Colorado, Amazon, Zambezi, Nile, Congo, Volga, Ganges, Yangtze.

Major cities, including Chicago, Toronto, Los Angeles, Lima, Buenos Aires, Caracas, Lagos, Johannesburg, Cairo, Jerusalem, St Petersburg, Delhi, Beijing, Tokyo, Singapore and Sydney.

The Oceans.

The Arctic and Antarctic Circles; the tropics of Cancer and Capricon; and the Equator.

★ describe what they would see if they were following a route on a detailed Ordnance Survey map (for example, churches, rivers, bridges etc).

★ use a map and a compass to follow a route around a park or wood.

★ explain different types of weathering and erosion.

★ explain the causes of rainfall.

★ explain why rivers, lakes and seas are vulnerable to pollution.

If your child is well above average, he or she may have reached *Level Seven* of the National Curriculum by this age. Amongst other things, children at this level would then be able to:

★ draw from an Ordnance Survey map an annotated sketch map showing relationships between human and physical features, e.g. the site and location of a town in relation to its physical setting.

★ interpret weather maps.

★ understand causes and effects of mass population movements (e.g. the migration of Jews to Israel).

At sixteen

At the age of 16 – after five years at secondary school – your child will probably be taking the GCSE. This examination also acts as the National Curriculum test for most pupils and, from 1994, it will be graded on the new ten-level scale.

The pupil of average ability should be around *Level Six* or *Seven*. This is roughly equivalent to the old GCSE grades E to C. To achieve this pupils should, amongst other things, be able to:

★ measure and record weather using thermometers, rain gauges, wind vanes etc.

★ describe the regions and features of their chosen European Community country.

★ describe the main energy sources in the USA, Japan, and the USSR.

★ describe the main characteristics of different types of climate/vegetation/landform.

★ compare economic development in different parts of the world, using measurements such as literacy levels and economic output, such as Gross Domestic Product per head of population.

★ explain global climatic changes, for example as a result of the increase in carbon dioxide levels.

The brightest pupils should be able to reach *Level Nine or Ten* of the National Curriculum. This is equivalent to the old-style GCSE grade A, with a Level Ten effectively worth an A plus. To achieve this, pupils should amongst other things be able to:

★ bring together information from Ordnance Survey, land-use, soil and conservation maps to produce a sketch map which highlights important geographical features and their relationships.

★ analyse recent trends in the pattern of international trade and suggest how they are likely to develop in future.

★ explain the global pattern of ocean currents and their climatic influences.

★ analyse the reasons for the distribution of ethnic groups in a city or a country.

★ explain the problems – such as pollution crossing international boundaries – faced by international efforts to protect the environment.

13
PHYSICAL
EDUCATION
■

WHAT IS PHYSICAL EDUCATION?
WHAT WILL MY CHILD BE TAUGHT?
WHAT WILL MY CHILD BE EXPECTED TO BE ABLE TO DO?

■ WHAT IS PHYSICAL EDUCATION?

For the first time, the National Curriculum requires all children from five to 16 who attend state schools to take part in a nationally agreed programme of physical education or PE as it it known. However pupils do not have to take a GCSE in the subject, although one is available.

Physical education and sport are not the same thing, although they do overlap. Sport covers the whole range of physical activities that people are involved in. It does not necessarily involve any elements of education. After-school team games, for example, are sport rather than PE. Physical education within the school timetable is specifically about learning through physical activity. The aim is to develop physical competence in a wide range of activities for all children, not just those who show particular ability in a specific sport.

PE's place in schools is perhaps more important than ever since out-of-hours sport has been in decline. A recent survery conducted by the Secondary Heads Association confirmed the trend for less and less sport after school and at weekends. There are several reasons for this decline, but perhaps the most important is that fewer teachers are now willing to give up their free time to run sports teams. They are not paid for this nor do they always receive expenses. The cost of maintaining sports facilities is another factor. Also many children have other interests or Saturday jobs which fill their time.

The survey also showed a similar decline in PE provision. It found that 70 per cent of 14-year-olds had less than the two hours of PE a week which the Secondary Heads Association recommends as a minimum. Many schools predicted that the demands of other parts of the National Curriculum would further erode time set aside for PE. The fact that PE is compulsory under the new curriculum may not be enough to protect it from this erosion, since a minimum time is not laid down for PE. According to Keith Smith, head teacher at Aylesbury Grammar School, as schools have strugged to fit the National Curriculum into their timetables, 'It has been a question of what can go. You cannot cut the mathematics, you cannot cut English, so people say let's cut the PE.'

In primary school, pupils must be taught a range of activities, including at least one from each of the following categories:

Athletics
Dance
Games
Gymnastics
Outdoor and Adventurous Activities
Swimming

In secondary school, pupils up to 14 must at some stage take part in activities in all of these areas, except swimming. Schools do not have to provide all of these activities for all of the time. But pupils in this age group are expected to cover at least four of the above areas during any one school year.

From 14 to 16, pupils who are not doing a GCSE in PE must take part in at least two different sporting activities. These could both be team games (soccer and cricket) or can be drawn from two different areas (such as hockey and gymnastics).

Swimming

The new curriculum requires schools to teach all youngsters to swim by the age of 11. However this requirement will not be enforced until the government is reassured it is feasible on cost grounds. This is an ambitious target since it is estimated that about one in five children fails to learn to swim. But it is important as an estimated 80 per cent of people who drown are non-swimmers.

The government was initially reluctant to accept this target because of concern over the costs involved. Most schools – especially primary schools – do not have their own swimming pools. Increased pool charges and the cost of transport have led many schools to reduce or end trips to their local municipal pools. Nevertheless, the target of requiring all 11-year-olds to be able to swim 25 metres has been accepted in principle by the government.

Outdoor education

Outdoor education covers activities on land and water and in the air. It can take place in both rural and urban settings. At its simplest it can cover young children learning to move around outdoor climbing frames or learning to orienteer within the school grounds. Older pupils may – if their school can offer such activities – be able to take part in canoeing, hill-walking and personal survival.

It is perhaps surprising to see outdoor education included in the National Curriculum as not all schools will have easy access to Outward Bound centres or to rivers, lakes, mountains and hills. However, a government survey showed that almost three-quarters of all primary schools and over half of all secondary schools said their pupils already took part in outdoor education. The survey also found that a majority of schools already made use of outdoor education centres. However most schools which were surveyed said that they would need extra money if outdoor education became compulsory. Although the final Parliamentary Order has yet to be passed, there is no sign that the government intends to drop this part of National Curriculum PE.

■ WHAT YOUR CHILD WILL BE TAUGHT

From five to seven

In the infant school children are expected to experience athletics, dance, gymnastics, games and outdoor/adventure activities. If the school does not teach swimming in the juniors, then they must teach it in the infants.

At this age, these activities should involve the following:

Athletics
This should include running, jumping and throwing with the aim of developing accuracy, speed and distance.

Dance
The aim is to develop control, balance and poise. Children should be able to explore moods and feelings through dance and learn how to respond to music.

Games
Children should be taught how to play with balls, learning to catch, throw, bounce and travel with balls of different sizes. Organised games should help children to learn to make up and follow rules and use equipment.

Gymnastics
Children should be taught actions such as climbing, rolling, swinging and balancing both on the floor and on apparatus.

Outdoor/adventure activities
Children should learn to develop skills on climbing frames or other playground equipment. They should also take part in simple orientation activities, such as finding their way around a local park or wood.

Swimming
Children should learn about water safety and how to recognise and avoid dangerous situations. Teachers will begin by teaching children to develop confidence in the water, before moving on to teach swimming strokes.

From seven to eleven
In the junior school, children should continue to take part in activities from all the main categories. However, primary schools do not have to teach swimming in the juniors if it has already been taught throughout the infants.

By the junior school most children will have already experienced most of the basic actions involved in PE and will now be ready to improve their performance through repetition. They will also begin to learn more about playing particular roles in teams and about good sporting behaviour. Teachers are expected to encourage children to analyse their own performance and to think of ways to improve it.

Athletics
Children should practise running over short and longer distances, including relays. They should also work at their jumping and throwing and take part in competitions.

Dance
Children should be taught to dance on their own, with partners and

in groups. They should be taught how to devise a beginning, middle and end to their dances and to develop a wider range of movement.

Games
Through different games – such as rounders – children will learn about attack and defence and develop their hitting and fielding abilities.

Gymnastics
Pupils should learn to put together in controlled sequences the sort of floor and apparatus movements they began at infant school.

Outdoor/adventure activities
By this age, pupils may be able to venture rather wider in their outdoor experience, which might include canoeing, camping, and walking depending on what is available. They should be taught about safety and how to avoid danger.

Swimming
As in the infant school, pupils should learn about water safety, to develop their confidence in the water (through floating and treading water), and how to swim on their front or back using recognised strokes. They will also be taught about personal survival skills and life-saving.

From 11 to 14
At secondary school there are specialist PE teachers and a wider range of facilites and equipment than in primary school. At this age, teaching will focus more on the quality of movement (for example, style of running, not just speed). There will also be more emphasis on the way youngsters plan and prepare for activities.

In any one year, pupils should take part in activities from at least four of the following areas and – over the three years – they must have taken part in all five:

Athletics
Pupils should be taught to take part in both explosive events (sprinting or long-jump, for example) as well as in activities requiring sustained effort. The aim is to develop their speed, strength, stamina and flexibility. Competitive swimming can be included within this category.

Dance

Pupils should be taught to perform set dances, to communicate ideas through movement and to match dance to music. They should also learn to recognise different styles of dance and to work out their own dance movements.

Games

Pupils should be taught different types of games, learning the rules and developing tactics. They should be taught to play different roles in these games and also to experience the role of umpire or referee.

Gymnastics

Using both floor and apparatus, pupils should develop their range of movements. They should begin to understand what contributes to good performance and to demonstrate aesthetic qualities in their movement.

Outdoor/adventure activities

Pupils should experience at least two types of outdoor activities (such as canoeing or climbing), learning the appropriate skills and recognising the potential hazards. They should be given a chance to lead activities as well as being a member of a team.

From 14 to 16

Pupils who are not taking PE to GCSE must still take part in at least two activities, although both can come from within a single category. Those who are taking GCSE will probably have to spend about as long on PE as on other GCSE subjects. They will be assessed not only on their performance but also on their theoretical knowledge and understanding through written coursework and examinations.

At this age, schools are encouraged to give pupils the widest possible choice of physical activity. This can include activities which take place outside the school and which prepare for the sort of sports they may take part in when they leave (squash or golf, for example).

Pupils should be taught about the structure and functions of the body, including nutritional needs, and the need for different types of exercise for good health. They should also be taught how to plan, monitor and improve their performance in their chosen activities.

Athletics

Pupils should learn how to set targets, to improve technniques and to prepare and follow training schedules. They should be taught the basic principles of aerobic and anaerobic training. Activities could include track and field events, cycling, swimming, rowing and cross-country running.

Dance

They should be taught to create dances and to perform more complex movements. They should also be shown how to design and choreograph dance productions.

Games

Pupils should learn how to train with others to improve performance. They should be taught to use and devise more advanced tactics and to learn how to adapt these to the strengths and weaknesses of individual players.

Gymnastics

Youngsters should be taught more advanced techniques, to design training programmes and learn the ways in which performance is judged. As well as the traditional gym-based activities, this category can include diving, synchronised swimming, martial arts, and trampolining.

Outdoor/adventure activities

Pupils should learn about the appropriate specialist equipment and clothing needed for activities and how to adapt to different types of weather and terrain. They should be taught how to plan and undertake a journey in an unfamiliar environment and to be aware of the effects on the body of exercise, nutrition and climatic conditions. The sort of activities that pupils might undertake include: canoeing, camping, caving, climbing, hill walking, mountaineering, orienteering, sailing, sub-aqua, and personal survival.

■ WHAT YOUR CHILD IS EXPECTED TO BE ABLE TO DO

The testing of your child's ability in PE is – not surprisingly – rather different from that in other National Curriculum subjects. With the exception of the GCSE, there will not be any nationally produced tests to measure achievement in PE. However, pupils will be assessed by their own teacher at seven, 11, 14 and 16. This will be largely based on activities observed over the year during normal lessons.

164

164

Pupils will not be judged on performance alone, although this will be the major element. Physical size and maturity will also be taken into account since children grow at different rates. Pupils' grasp of style, skills and tactics will be judged as well as their physical ability. Correct preparation – including selection of warm-up exercises and appropriate equipment – and the ability to analyse performance will also be assessed.

At seven

At the end of the infant school, children should be able to show they can perform single and linked sequences of movements, practise and improve their performance and recognise the effects of exercise on their bodies. As a guide, an average seven-year-old should be at *Level Two* which means they should be able to:

★ move under/over/through apparatus.

★ keep a regular rhythm while skipping or dancing.

★ bounce a large ball with alternate hands.

★ understand simple rules, like stopping when the whistle is blown.

Seven-year-olds who are progressing more quickly may reach *Level Three*, which means they are able to:

★ receive, travel with a ball and pass it to a partner.

★ use simple tactics, such as feigning a hard hit or throw but making a gentle one.

★ recognise changes in heart rate.

At eleven

By the end of primary school, the average 11-year-old should have reached *Level Four* and should be able to:

★ swim at least 25 metres and understand water safety.

★ memorise and repeat a series of movements, such as a dance or gymnastics sequence.

★ know how to evaluate and improve performance, e.g. concentrating on height and style when trampolining.

★ adapt movement or dance to the mood of a piece of music.

★ understand how to prepare for physical activity, e.g. by warming up properly.

At fourteen

By 14, the average pupil should have reached around *Level Five* or *Six*. As a general guide, this means they should, amongst other things, be able to:

★ refine athletic skills (for example, race turns in swimming).
★ select and apply team tactics (such as setting field placings in cricket or rounders).
★ sustain an idea throughout a dance.
★ create and perform a dance or a gymnastics sequence.
★ carry out tasks in potentially hazardous conditions, for example outdoor activities in changing weather conditions.
★ plan a programme for developing skills (for example, learning to throw the discus).

At sixteen
Some pupils will choose to take a GCSE in physical education. As GCSE papers are adapted to fit the National Curriculum, it is thought likely that there will be two kinds of GCSE. One will based on a general course, with several activities. The other is likely to have a specialised focus, for example on dance, outdoor education or sports studies. However, the examination authorities have not yet decided these matters.

At 16 the average pupil should – in their chosen activities – be achieving *Level Six* or *Seven*. That means they should be able to:
★ perform consistently (for example, when serving in tennis or bowling in cricket).
★ take a variety of different roles (such as umpire, coach, player, defender, attacker, team captain).
★ create a composition in dance, gymnastics, swimming, or trampolining.
★ organise a schedule or activities suitable for different individuals.

More able pupils who are at *Level Nine* or *Ten* should be able to show 'outstanding practical ability, knowledge and understanding' in at least two activities of their choice.

14
MUSIC
.

WHAT DOES MUSIC INVOLVE?
WHAT WILL MY CHILD STUDY?
WHAT WILL MY CHILD BE EXPECTED TO KNOW?

■ WHAT DOES MUSIC INVOLVE?

We all have different views on what is – or is not – music. One person's favourite sounds can be another's idea of an unpleasant noise. The National Curriculum has tried to avoid getting caught in this sort of argument and does not specify in any great detail the sort of music that children should be introduced to. This has annoyed those who believe it should stress the role of classical composers such as Beethoven, Mozart or Bach rather than modern pop music. But the experts who devised the new music curriculum say that it is up to individual teachers to choose the most appropriate musical repertoire for their pupils.

However, the new curriculum does say children should study music of different styles and from different periods and cultures, including composers who have shaped the language of music. It says this should include a balanced selection from each of the following:

★ the European 'classical' tradition.
★ folk and popular music.
★ music of the regions of the British Isles.
★ other musical traditions and cultures.

The National Curriculum makes music compulsory for all pupils from five to 14. This is a big change since – although most schools provided some music – it has often been taught in a very limited way until now. The National Curriculum should provide a broader approach to music for all schools, although this hinges on there being enough teachers qualified in the subject. While only a small number of children will go on to enter the music profession, there are many jobs where a knowledge of music is useful. These include posts in broadcasting, the recording industry, music publishing, and concert hall management. Above all, though, an introduction to music at school will enrich adult life.

Until now the most common element of music in primary schools has been singing. In a few schools this has been the only music available. Most, though, use percussion instruments (drums, tambourines, triangles and so on) and many teach children to play the recorder. This is a very good way of introducing children to play a musical instrument. For many it will lead on to other instruments. So – however squeaky the initial sounds – do encourage your children to play the recorder at home. Recorders are not expensive so, if it is difficult for children to bring them home from school, it could be worth buying one. As with all instrument-playing, persistent practice is needed if it is to be mastered.

By the junior school, pupils may well be able to attempt a wider variety of musical instruments and should also be able to take part in ensemble music-playing. The new curriculum will give a boost to composing in primary schools. That may sound rather ambitious, but 'composing' is used in its widest sense to include improvisation as well as writing musical scores.

In secondary schools, music takes up around five per cent of the timetable and it is usually taught by specialist teachers. A fairly small proportion of pupils are also taught to play musical instruments, usually by visiting instrument teachers employed by the local education authority. Sadly, this service has been one of the first to be cut in several areas recently as councils have been forced to make priorities in their education spending.

Music is mainly a practical activity. The new curriculum identifies three main areas of musical skills:

Performing
This ranges from clapping, singing and humming – which even the youngest children can do – to developing dexterity with instruments, reading music and giving performances.

Composing
This includes both improvising and more formal arranging. Younger children will learn how to vary rhythm and melodic pattern while older pupils will learn how to control and manipulate musical patterns in more sophisticated ways.

Appraising
This involves developing the ability to listen attentively to music and to criticise and evaluate it. Older pupils should also be able to follow musical scores while listening to music.

■ WHAT YOUR CHILD WILL STUDY
From five to seven
Few of us give much thought to the way we listen to music. But listening is as important a skill as playing music. Indeed it is essential to listen attentively before you can play, particularly when accompanying others. So listening is one of the first skills children will be taught to develop. They will learn how to recognise and describe variations in sound, such as high/low, fast/slow, or loud/quiet.

Once they have begun to recognise variations in pitch and rhythm they will then apply these in their own music-making. They will learn how to make music using their own body, clapping, singing, humming and so on. Most schools will have a range of percussion instruments as well. Children can also make their own percussion instruments, something parents can help them do at home. Toilet roll centres filled with rice or dried peas make good maracas!

Children will be taught the disciplines of music, such as how to start and stop on command, with the teacher or perhaps another child acting as a conductor. Building on what they have observed by listening, they should learn how to make high or low sounds and how to set a fast or a slow rhythm. As they get more proficient they should learn to recognise and repeat a musical pattern or phrase.

Once children have learnt the basic ingredients that make up music they can start to create their own compositions. Improvising and composing are now an important part of music in the infants school. The two go together. Teachers may show children how to record their own improvisations and then to play them back and to discuss each other's work.

Using very simple visual symbols (for example a large symbol for a loud sound and a small one for a quieter sound) children of this age can even be taught to devise a musical score. This type of written music – called a 'graphic score' – is a first step towards using standard musical notation (quavers, crotchets and so on). These graphic scores can be devised by children or teachers using a 'key' as in a map. High or low pitch or fast or slow rhythms can be denoted by a range of symbols such as geometrical shapes, colours, or drawings.

Having learnt how to listen to and make music, children should also be given the chance to develop their responses to music. So, for example, they might be asked to move or dance to music or to paint a picture reflecting the mood and feeling of a piece of music. In doing all this, they should learn how to express their own likes and dislikes in music and to give reasons explaining their preferences.

From seven to eleven
In the juniors, children will be taught to use rather more precise terms to describe variations in music. So, for example, they will learn about: melody, accompaniment, chords, metre, and rhythm.

They will be taught to develop their musical skills, for example listening to and singing back longer musical phrases. They should also learn the correct playing techniques for percussion instruments and how to play with others to produce a performance.

At this stage your child should be listening to music from a wide variety of styles and periods. They should also learn to recognise and group different instruments, including brass, wind and strings.

From 11 to 14
In the secondary school, your child will be taught how to listen to increasingly complex music and to recognise detailed musical elements, such as: melodic and harmonic intervals, scales, time signatures, syncopation, verse/chorus, and rondo. They should also learn how to follow a simple score while listening to music.

In their music-making, they should be learning how to read music and how to rehearse with others. They might also learn to improvise in different styles, for example over a 12-bar blues.

During this time, pupils should be introduced to a wide variety of different types of music. The National Curriculum gives – as an example – the following: a baroque concerto movement, romantic opera aria, folk song, African drumming, jazz and music in the pop-charts.

From 14 to 16
Those opting for music after 14 can choose between taking a full GCSE course or taking a short course in music alone or combined with another subject.

At this age, the approach becomes more detailed and precise but is still built around the three main areas of performing, composing, and appraising, with pupils expected to do the following:

Performing
★ to a high standard with voice or instrument.
★ by ear and from written music.
★ for an audience from their own and others' compositions.

Composing
★ through improvisation in a variety of styles.
★ writing down compositions using correct notation.
★ devising compositions using formal musical structures.
★ inventing original musical ideas.

Appraising
★ listening to a broad range of music and relating it to its historical and cultural setting.
★ critically appraising musical performances.
★ following a score for four or more instruments.

■ WHAT YOUR CHILD IS EXPECTED TO KNOW
Children will not take formal, nationally set tests in music unless they choose to take a GCSE in the subject. So the assessments of children's performance will be made mainly by their own class teacher. This will be heavily based on practical music-making. For younger children this can often be done while children are singing or playing in groups.

At the time of writing, the arrangements for music in the National Curriculum have not yet been finalised. What follows may change by the time final approval is given by the government. Nevertheless, they give parents an idea of the sort of knowledge and abilities expected of children at different ages.

At seven
By seven, the child of average ability should be at *Level Two* on the National Curriculum ten-point scale. To achieve this they should – amongst other things – be able to do the following:
★ sing a variety of songs with clarity and expression, either individually or with others.
★ accompany a song with regular instrumental sound patterns.
★ produce simple sound patterns with voice, clapping or simple instrument.
★ represent sound patterns using visual symbols.

Children who have reached *Level Three* should amongst other things be able to:
★ listen to a melody, sing it silently, then aloud.
★ show increasing control when singing, for example deciding where to breathe to make sense of a phrase.
★ to play music from visual symbols that denote rhythm or degrees of volume.
★ compose a piece which has a beginning, middle and end.

At eleven
By the end of the junior school, the average child should be at *Level Four* on the ten-point scale of the National Curriculum. To achieve this they should be able to:
★ perform a part within a score made up of simple symbols using shapes and colours.
★ perform songs with increasing control of tone quality.
★ make a graphic score of a composition.
★ identify different instruments while listening to a piece of music.

At fourteen
After three years at secondary school, the average child should be at *Level Five* or *Six* on the National Curriculum scale. To achieve this they should be able to:
★ perform – for example, on a recorder – in a range of musical styles.
★ sing and play in groups, where individual parts are performed separately from others.
★ perform a short solo passage.
★ sight-read a simple musical passage for voice or instrument.
★ compose a piece within particular melodic or rhythmic styles, such as a 'rap'.
★ identify chord changes or rhythmic patterns when listening to music.

At sixteen
This is the only stage at which pupils will take nationally-set tests in music – and then only if they are taking a GCSE. From 1994, the current GCSE A to G grades will convert to the National Curriculum levels 10 to 4. The average 16-year-old should be at around *Level Six* (equivalent to a D/E at GCSE) or *Level Seven* (grade C/D). To achieve this they should be able to:
★ perform a piece of music which they are seeing for the first time.

★ plan and present a performance of their own work.

★ compose in different musical forms, for example a piece to accompany Elizabethan drama.

★ recognise and describe music from different periods in history or from different cultures.

★ analyse individual timbres, textures, harmonies and patterns in different types of music.

★ demonstrate knowledge of musical notation and an ability to read a classical music score.

Pupils who have reached *Level Nine or Ten* – equivalent to GCSE grade A or A+ – should amongst other things be able to do some of the following (or similar activities of comparable difficulty):

★ perform a wide and demanding repertoire of pieces, such as performing in a gospel choir, playing in a string quartet or improvising in a jazz group.

★ demonstrate a high level of skill in a solo performance.

★ produce compositions with a high level of technical skills and a sense of style, e.g. select and arrange instrumental music for a school production.

★ make a detailed critical appraisal of music of a variety of styles, periods and types.

15
ART

■

WHAT DOES ART INVOLVE?

WHAT WILL MY CHILD STUDY?

WHAT WILL MY CHILD BE EXPECTED TO KNOW?

■ WHAT DOES ART INVOLVE?

Art is now compulsory for all children from five to 14. Many people were delighted when both art and music were included in the National Curriculum. It seemed to lend a new importance to the Arts which are often neglected by many pupils in secondary schools. But there was disappointment when, later, the government indicated that both subjects would be optional for pupils after 14 because of the overcrowding of school timetables.

Nevertheless, the National Curriculum will broaden the way art is taught in those schools which until now had concentrated mainly on drawing and painting. Many youngsters still leave school after only the narrowest introduction to art. They may never have been given the chance to find out about textiles, ceramics, sculpture, fashion and jewellery design, photography and computer-aided design. This is a pity, for they can enrich youngsters' visual appreciation of the world around us and – more practically – they are useful in very many jobs.

According to the government's advisers, art is important because children today 'learn as much through visual images as they do through words . . . and they need to learn that pictures and symbols can have several meanings'. In short, what can be called visual literacy is a very important skill in modern life when we are bombarded daily with images on television, film, advertising hoardings and in newspapers, magazines and promotional literature.

On average, primary school children do art for a little under two hours a week. In the early years at secondary school it is not much more than one hour a week. In primary schools, art is usually taught by your child's class teacher who is unlikely to be an art specialist. In secondary school your child will probably be taught by someone specifically trained in the subject. The National Curriculum is unlikely to mean more time for art, but it should mean more youngsters continuing with it for longer and a wider use of different techniques and materials.

The National Curriculum does not separate art and crafts, as has sometimes beeen the case. Rather it recognises that craft skills can be part of the process of realising ideas in art and design. In other words, just knowing how to do something makes new ideas possible.

The stated aims for art in the new curriculum include:

★ developing creative and technical skills.
★ developing imaginative and original thought.
★ developing ideas and abilities in design.
★ teaching pupils to become visually literate.

National Curriculum art covers three main aspects of the subject. These are:

Understanding
Pupils should be taught to appreciate the work and methods of artists, designers and craftworkers. They will also compare work in different cultures.

Making
This covers the practical skills and knowledge which pupils need to develop in order to express their ideas through art. They will learn about different artistic tools, materials and techniques.

Investigating
This involves developing pupils' visual perception, by encouraging them to improve their skills of observation and recording. It is also about learning to use reference materials, to look up examples of artists' work in order to clarify and develop ideas for their own work.

■ WHAT YOUR CHILD WILL STUDY
For art – unlike some other subjects – the National Curriculum pro-vides only a very broad outline of what children should be doing. Teachers are free to choose different activities to achieve the same aims.

From five to seven

In the infant school, children should be experimenting with a range of different ways of drawing, painting and making things. As well as using pencils, crayons and paint they will be shaping clay or weaving as well as making collages using different items, such as leaves, shells and straws.

At this age, children should be starting to learn about line and tone, for example learning how to use a thick soft pencil or crayon for the fuzzy lines of a teddy bear and a hard pencil or fine felt-tip pen for the sharper detail of a toy tractor. They should also be starting to experiment with colours, perhaps by mixing them to try to match the colours of autumn leaves.

They should be encouraged to think about shape and form by drawing familiar objects from different viewpoints and by working together to make things out of different materials as part of classroom themes.

Teachers will also encourage children to start making comparisons between their own work and the work of well-known artists. They will be encouraged to observe and talk about the art and design they see around them at home and in school, for example discussing different designs for teapots or hats. They can then go on to make their own designs for these items or to design and make their own birthday/Christmas/Easter cards.

From seven to eleven

By the junior school, children should be introduced to a wider range of artist's materials and techniques to explore further line, tone, colour and texture. These might include trying different ways of printing, sketching with charcoal, and making collages with natural objects.

In comparing their work with that of professional artists, they should be encouraged to talk about specific approaches, such as the way different painters have represented the sky or the sea.

Looking at other visual forms – such as portraits, posters, or television commercials – children will learn to recognise that there are different kinds or art and design for different purposes. They should start to consider how design has evolved over the years, looking perhaps at changes in costume and fashion over the centuries.

Teachers are expected to encourage children's powers of observation. This might be done by making drawings around the school from different perspectives (worm's eye view, bird's eye view or a view through a window or a door). They should also be encouraged to use sketch-books to record their observations, perhaps by keeping a visual record of a school visit or field trip.

From 11 to 14
In the secondary school, pupils will be introduced to a wide range of materials and techniques, learning how best to use them to express their ideas and to convey meaning. Some recommended activities include:

★ designing and printing a poster on an issue of public concern.

★ transforming everyday objects into other images.

★ making objects or sculptures using unconventional materials, like wireflex or plastic sheeting.

★ designing jewellery.

By now, pupils should be starting to analyse the work of major artists, recognising different methods and 'schools'. They should be able to use and understand terms such as: abstract, symbolic, expressionist, cubist. They should also be learning about art from other periods and cultures.

From 14 to 16
By this stage those youngsters who have opted to continue with art should be looking more rigorously at connections between their own work and that of well-known artists and designers. They should learn how to borrow and adapt the methods of influential artists by, for example:

★ designing an interior recognising the influence of designers such as Charles Rennie Mackintosh or Laura Ashley.

★ making urban studies on the theme of 'Outcasts', referring to the work of artists such as Hogarth or Don McCullin.

★ designing a pictorial alphabet drawing on the work of well-known illustrators.

Pupils will learn how to improve their use of different materials and techniques in drawing, painting and sculpture. They should develop their skills of observation by, for example, doing a series of studies of local buildings of architectural interest using maps, diagrams, plans and photographs. Other activities might include:

★ making three-dimensional heads using wire.

★ developing techniques with paint, print, ceramics.

★ work with water-colours, learning techniques such as graded washes and wet-into-wet.

They should also learn to analyse the ways design is used to influence moods and opinions. This could include looking at the impact of posters and signs and comparing different television commercials.

■ WHAT YOUR CHILD IS EXPECTED TO KNOW

Clearly, testing in art is bound to be different from more academic subjects. There is not the same wealth of factual information which can be assessed by written tests. It is much more about combining knowledge and skills. So there will not be any Standard Assessment Tasks in art. All assessment – except the GCSE – will be carried out by teachers. They will usually assess children on the way they work and on what they produce, such as a term's project in primary school.

At the time of writing, the details of National Curriculum art have still to be finalised. The examples of what children are expected to be able to do are taken from the latest proposals and give a guide to the sort of knowledge and abilities expected of pupils at different ages.

At seven

By the end of the infants, the average seven-year-old should be at around *Level Two* on the National Curriculum ten-level scale. To achieve this, they should be able to:

★ make connections between their own work and that of famous artists, for example drawing children in the park after discussing L.S. Lowry's paintings of figures in similar settings.
★ make a picture from rubbings from different surfaces, recognising rough and smooth textures.
★ design a hat appropriate to a particular occasion.
★ use different drawing methods, such as charcoal for a 'fantasy' drawing of a beast and sharp pencil or biro for a detailed drawing of sections of fruit.

More able pupils who reach *Level Three* should be able to:
★ design their own sweet wrapper.
★ practise colour mixing and select appropriately sized brushes for a portrait.
★ make drawings recording the growth of plants in the classroom over several weeks.

At eleven

By the end of junior school, the average 11-year-old should have reached *Level Four* on the National Curriculum scale. To achieve this they should be able to:

★ make use of comparisons with the work of well-known artists to improve their own, for example painting trees in blossom after looking at works by Palmer and Monet.

★ show an understanding of art in other cultures by, for example, looking at the different ways the human face is depicted in art from different times and places.

★ show a command of different techniques and materials, by choosing appropriate means to depict different aspects of birds or animals.

★ make quick 'on-the-spot' drawings of the classroom and then using graph paper and rulers develop scale-drawings of the room.

At fourteen

By the age of 14, pupils should be able to make use of the approaches and methods used by other artists and designers and should be able to make appropriate choices of materials and techniques.

The average pupil should have reached *Level Five* or *Level Six*. To achieve this they should be able to:

★ make incised prints of an imaginary landscape after looking at the work of professional print-makers.

★ contrast familiar artefacts (lamps or woven fabrics, for example) from different times and cultures.

★ make a collage version of famous period paintings.

★ make a weaving based on the study of plant forms, selecting appropriate coloured and sized wools.

★ make a lino-print using different colours and different paper textures.

★ devise a story-board for a slide/tape sequence or cartoon.

★ collect and organise different typefaces from newspapers and then design a mast head and banner headlines for a school newspaper.

At sixteen

Pupils who have chosen to continue with art after 14 may also choose to take a GCSE in the subject. From 1994, the current G to A grades at GCSE will become levels 4 to 10 on the National Curriculum scale.

By this age pupils should be able to incorporate into their own work methods they have studied in the work of well-known artists. They should know about different art forms and should be able to place art in its historical and cultural context.

Pupils of average ability are expected to reach half way between *Level Six* and *Level Seven*. This is roughly equivalent to a grade D. To achieve this, pupils should – amongst other things – be able to do the following:

★ discuss the different ways artists have represented journeys.

★ design and make a wall-hanging in mixed media, referring to artists such as Jackson Pollock.

★ block-print a fashion fabric based on designs generated through a computer.

★ discuss and review drawings and notes made on a visit to a local site and select the material most appropriate to follow-up work.

★ devise body-painting designs for characters in *A Midsummer Night's Dream*.

To achieve *Level Nine* or *Level Ten* – the equivalent to an A grade at GCSE – pupils should be able to:

★ use the work of other artists to benefit their own work, for example when designing the setting for a school production.

★ understand the methods and approaches used by artists, craftworkers and designers, for example the handling of space, scale and mass in the architectural studies of Piranesi, Masereel and Creffield.

★ establish personal methods for their own making of images, for example designing and painting a mural for a public space.

★ modify their work to fit the target audience, for example designing and making a children's book.

★ use a variety of methods for recording perceptions or ideas, for example drawing and photographing a room from different angles and under different lighting conditions.

16
CHOICES AT SIXTEEN
■

SCHOOL, COLLEGE OR TRAINING?

A AND A/S LEVELS

OTHER COURSES

■ SCHOOL, COLLEGE OR TRAINING?

At present the National Curriculum ends when pupils reach 16. That is also the age at which youngsters can leave school. Whether they intend to stay at school or not, they now face an important, and difficult, choice of routes to continue their education or training. It is always worth turning to schools, colleges or the local careers advisory service (run by your local authority) for help. They will be happy to give you advice and information.

GCSE results come out around the middle of August – just in time to make or break summer holidays! Most youngsters and their parents will have decided what they plan to do before the results arrive. But results better or worse than expected could cause a change of plans. It is not too late to decide to return to school or college to re-take GCSEs or to take A levels or some other qualifications such as vocational courses (see pages 184–6).

For most youngsters the decision about where to study will be closely tied to the qualifications they want to take. But before looking at the details of different courses, what is the choice of places to study at 16? The most obvious is to stay at school and enter the sixth-form, either for A Levels or to repeat GCSEs. But in areas where schools are organised on an 11 to 16 basis, then some sort of change is inevitable. The straightforward route then is to the local sixth-form college or tertiary college. Although rather an ugly name, tertiary simply means third-stage. In other words, it is the next step after the primary and secondary stages of education.

Most students at sixth-form and tertiary colleges will be doing A Levels, but as with school-based sixth forms there are other options (see pages 184–6). Further Education (FE) colleges are another choice. They too offer both academic and vocational courses. Of course, pupils may choose to switch to these colleges even when their own school does have a sixth-form. Equally, it is quite possible simply to change from one school to another at the start of the sixth-form. Pupils who failed to get into a grammar school at 11 but who have done well at GCSE may be able to make the switch at this stage. It is also common for pupils to move into or away from the independent sector at this stage.

The choice between school, sixth-form college and FE college will depend on students' own views on their preferred surroundings. Staying at school has the advantage that youngsters will have less trouble settling in as they already know the teachers and the buildings. They may also gain something from their new-found position of responsibility at the top of the school, perhaps helping to organise activities for younger pupils. Schools will usually have a greater sense of community than colleges. Most schools also loosen their rules – on uniform or compulsory sport, for example – for sixth-formers. On the other hand, a college may offer greater freedom and a more adult atmosphere away from younger children. There will probably be fewer rules and may well be a wider range of courses and qualifications.

WHERE TO GO AT 16?
- stay at school and enter sixth-form.
- change from one school to another.
- go to separate sixth-form/tertiary college.
- go to Further Education college.
- take a Youth Training place.
- enter full-time employment.

The latest figures show that in England and Wales just over half of all 16-year-olds stay in education. A further 17 per cent continue with some form of part-time study on Youth Training courses and another 17 per cent go straight into employment. The remainder are either unemployed or their status is not known.

Youth training

Youth Training offers school-leavers a two-year course with an employer coupled with the chance to attend college on a part-time basis. The aim is to provide both on-the-job experience and formal training. Trainees receive an allowance. There is a government commitment to provide a Youth Training place for all 16 to 18-year-olds who want one. You can find out about the scheme from your local careers office.

The government is currently developing a scheme of training 'credits'. These will be issued to school-leavers by Training and Enterprise Councils. Youngsters will then be able to present these credits to an employer or a college in exchange for training. The first credits – or vouchers – were issued to school leavers in 1991 in selected areas of the country. However, it remains to be seen how far this pilot scheme will develop.

■ A AND A/S LEVELS

A Levels

Advanced Levels are two-year academic courses. Students will usually need four or five GCSE passes at grade C or above to go on to A Level, although many places have no specific entry requirements. A Levels are the main qualification needed by students who want to go to university, polytechnic or Higher Education college to take degree courses. However they may not be the best option for all youngsters. They are very demanding, represent a big change of gear after GCSEs, and the drop-out and failure rate is quite high.

The traditional pattern has been for students to take three A Levels, although a choice of two or four is not uncommon. Students tend to take either all arts subjects or all sciences, although this is certainly not a requirement. Indeed for a long time there has been concern that most A Level students are studying too narrow a range of subjects. Our academically-minded 16 to 18-year-olds certainly take a narrower range of subjects than most of their European counterparts.

There have been proposals to reform A Levels so students can take five or more subjects as a matter of course, but so far these have come to nothing. However, one recent reform has attempted to broaden students' studies without changing the nature of A Levels. This has involved the creation of a new examination, the Advanced Supplementary or A/S Level.

At A Level there are some 60 different courses, including many subjects which pupils will not have been able to do before. They range from accounting to zoology. Not all schools and colleges will be able to offer the full range of options. But in addition to continuing with subjects taken in the National Curriculum before 16, pupils may be able to do A Levels in subjects as varied as theatre studies, sociology, law, economics, psychology, computer studies or history of art, to name just a few.

Youngsters who are thinking of going on to take a degree course should find out about entry qualifications before selecting their A Level courses. Some degree courses will require specific A Levels. Those who are uncertain what degree course they want to take, may be well advised to stick with fairly mainstream A Level subjects, rather than something very specific like theatre studies. You can find out about particular requirements by consulting *University Entrance, The Official Guide* which is updated each year and should be available in libraries.

A/S Levels

Advanced Supplementary Levels are still relatively new and many employers and parents are uncertain what they involve. They are two-year academic courses with about half the content of an A Level. They therefore take up about half the teaching time of a full A Level. But they are of the same academic difficulty as the A Level, and are graded from A to E in the same way. In other words, an A/S Level is an A Level split in half vertically, not horizontally.

SOME POSSIBLE A AND A/S CHOICES			
	Traditional Choice A Level	*Broader A/S Choice* A Level	A/S Level
Science student	Maths Physics Chemistry	Maths Physics	Chemistry English
Arts student	English History French	English History	French Computing

The aim is for students to replace the standard three A Levels with two A Levels and two A/S Levels. But these courses have not caught on as quickly as the government hoped. This is partly because some say two A/S Levels do take up more time than one A Level. Nor have they always broadened students' approach, with many youngsters preferring to take A/S Levels in subjects similar to their main A Level choices.

■ OTHER COURSES
The International Baccalaureate

This is an alternative to A Levels which is based on the rather broader approach common in many other countries in Europe. It is run by the International Baccalaureate Organisation in Geneva which was created in the mid-1960s through cooperation between a number of international schools. The IB diploma is taught by some 350 schools in around 60 countries – including several in Britain – and is recognised for entry to most degree courses.

The main difference the IB offers over A Levels is its breadth. Pupils usually take six subjects in all, three at a higher level and three subsidiaries. These must cover subjects across the whole range, including the arts, sciences, humanities and a foreign language. Pupils must also do an extended essay – involving research work – of around 4,000 words.

According to Colin Jenkins, principal of Atlantic College in South Glamorgan – an independent sixth-form college which teaches the IB –the broad approach 'does not lead to the dropping of studies in very important areas and it also maintains a whole range of skills much wider than A Level.' Students at Atlantic College seem to agree. According to James Tansey, taking six subjects 'means I can keep my options open right up until university.'

The IB is mainly available in international or independent schools and some colleges of further education. There are exceptions to this, such as the Ingatestone Anglo-European School in Essex and Impington Village College in Cambridgeshire, both of which are state schools taking pupils from 11 to 18.

Further information on the International Baccalaureate can be obtained from its UK office at: Pascal Close, St Mellons, Cardiff, Wales, CF3 0YP. Tel: 0222–770770.

Vocational courses

Youngsters who do not want to follow an academic course – or who already have a clear idea of what sort of employment they want to enter – can choose from a range of vocational courses, many of which are now available in schools as well as colleges.

Vocational courses are mainly taken by students with one to four GCSEs at grade C or above, or with five or more GCSEs at lower grades. In the past the vocational route has been seen by many as second best. Much is being done to change this peculiarly British snobbery about vocational courses but attitudes are hard to alter. Youngsters who do not want to go on to degree courses – and who have a clear idea of their career direction – may well find these courses more useful than A Levels. Also they do not necessarily close the door to university or polytechnic.

BTEC

Courses approved by the Business and Technology Education Council (BTEC) are available in colleges of further education, through company training schemes and – increasingly – in schools. They are vocational courses covering areas such as: agriculture, business, computing, construction, design, engineering, health and social care, hotel and catering, science, and travel and tourism. They can be taken full-time or on day-release. They offer a more practical approach than A Levels, but they cover theory too.

BTEC courses are made up of units covering different subjects, with a core of compulsory subjects. They often involve some work experience. There are three main levels – First, National and Higher National – although only the first two are suitable for 16-year-olds.

BTEC FIRST DIPLOMA
- broadly equivalent to GCSEs.
- one year full-time or two years part-time.
- no formal entry requirement, but some colleges prefer GCSEs.
- leads to employment or to BTEC National.

BTEC NATIONAL DIPLOMA
- broadly equivalent to A Level.
- two years full-time or three years part-time.
- entry requirement: 4 GCSEs at grade C or above or BTEC First.
- leads to employment or higher education.

CPVE

The Certificate of Pre-Vocational Education is for youngsters who do not want to do A Levels and who still do not have a very clear idea of what area of work they want to go into. It is a one-year course and no previous qualifications are needed. It is available in school sixth-forms and colleges of further education and can be combined with GCSEs. The CPVE is also available as part of Youth Training courses.

The idea of the CPVE is to give students a chance to sample several different types of work while giving them the basic skills they will eventually need in employment. Students can choose to work on a number of different areas, such as business administration, computing, construction, engineering, hairdressing, health and community care, and retailing. The core skills covered include communication, numeracy, social skills, information technology and problem-solving.

The CPVE is administered by the City and Guilds Institute, which intends gradually to replace it with a new Diploma of Vocational Education. This will have two levels: Intermediate for one-year courses and National for two-year courses. It will continue to combine both core and vocational skills.

City and Guilds

City and Guilds certificates are vocational qualifications in specific technical subjects. They are available at colleges of further education. Courses are offered in more than 300 subjects, including agriculture, engineering, furniture, information technology, hotel and catering, mining, retailing, textiles, travel, tourism and recreation.

The Royal Society of Arts also offers specific vocational courses at colleges of further education. They cover commercial subjects, including secretarial courses teaching shorthand and typing.

Addresses:

Business and Technology Education Council (BTEC), Central House, Upper Woburn Place, London WC1H 0HH. Tel: 071–388–3288.

City and Guilds of London Institute, 76 Portland Place, London W1N 4AA. Tel: 071–580–3050.

Royal Society of Arts (RSA), 8 John Adam Street, London WC2N 6AJ. Tel: 071–930–5115.

17
YOUR RIGHTS
AS A PARENT
■

FREE EDUCATION?

YOUR RIGHT TO INFORMATION

YOUR RIGHT TO CHOOSE

HOW TO COMPLAIN

RELIGION

SPECIAL NEEDS

■ FREE EDUCATION – OR IS IT?

Your most important right as a parent is access to a free school place for your child. The law requires local education authorities to make sure there are enough school places in the area to meet demand. Specifically, they must offer a free school place to children from the beginning of the term following their fifth birthday. However, there is no right to a free place in a nursery class or school. Education before five is entirely at the discretion of local authorities. The availability of places in nursery schools or classes varies enormously from one area of the country to another.

What can schools charge for?

Despite the right to a free school place, there are some things for which schools can charge parents. The 1988 Education Reform Act aimed to ensure that no children were put at a disadvantage because their parents could not afford to pay for activities or visits linked to their basic education. Unfortunately, this has created confusion over exactly what schools are allowed to charge for.

Visits to museums, farms, zoos, theatres and residential field centres are a common feature of school life which add interest and understanding to aspects of the curriculum. Unfortunately many schools can only afford to provide such activities if the money comes from parents. In the past, schools could charge parents all or part of the cost. If some parents could not afford to pay then usually the school would pay for them from other funds.

But now the law says schools cannot charge parents for any activity undertaken in school hours. The only exception is for individual musical instrument tuition and even this cannot be charged for if it is part of a syllabus leading to a public examination. There cannot even be a charge for activities which take place partly outside school hours if more than half of the time falls within school time or if it is part of the National Curriculum or an examination syllabus. Parents can, or course, still be invited to make voluntary contributions towards activities, providing children are free to take part whether or not their parents have contributed.

MAINTAINED SCHOOLS CANNOT REQUIRE PAYMENT FOR

- admission to the school.
- examination entry fees, unless the subject is not taught at the school.
- books or equipment required for normal school activities.
- activities relating to the National Curriculum or to an examination syllabus.
- most activities where at least half the duration (including travel) falls within school hours.
- transport to and from visits away from school.
- entrance fees to museums, theatres etc.

MAINTAINED SCHOOLS CAN CHARGE FOR

- individual musical instrument tuition, unless it forms part of an examination syllabus, e.g. A Level music.
- board and lodging on school trips.
- examination fees if the pupil fails to turn up without good reason.
- materials such as cooking ingredients if the pupil wishes to take home anything they make and it is not part of an examination syllabus.
- activities which take place mainly outside school hours and which are not related to an examination syllabus.

Independent schools are, of course, free to charge parents for whatever they think necessary. When choosing a fee-paying school, it is worth asking about the costs of 'extras', such as music tuition, books, medical supplies and craft materials.

Can I get help with costs?

The answer to this is yes, but it is up to your local education authority how much to give, what for and to whom. Grants are sometimes available for clothing, school trips, and transport. Free school meals are only available to those on income support.

You can find out what is available from your local education authority. The address and telephone number will be in the directory or you can ask at your local library. If you are not getting a grant to which you think you are entitled you have the right to complain to the Secretary of State for Education.

■ YOUR RIGHT TO INFORMATION

You have the right to state your choice of school, but first you need access to information about local schools as a basis for making that choice. Parents now have considerable rights in this area.

Local education authorities must give you a list of all their schools, with addresses and telephone numbers. They must also tell you about the types of school available and about admissions arrangements. In future – if the Conservative government carries through its 'Parent's Charter' – education authorities will have to give comparable information on all schools in the locality, including independent schools and grant-maintained schools. They may also be required to publish performance tables showing examination scores, truancy rates and where their school-leavers go on to.

WHAT SCHOOLS MUST TELL YOU
- how you can visit to find out more.
- the curriculum for different age groups.
- arrangements for pupils with special educational needs.
- the way the school is organised.
- policy on discipline, uniform, homework and sex education.
- the main activities which take place outside school hours.
- policy on entry to examinations.
- examination results in full and according to a standard format.

Individual schools must publish prospectuses giving the aims of the school, the subjects and activities offered, and rates of truancy and examination success. You also have the right to see any report by Her Majesty's Inspectors of Schools and the annual report from the school's governors.

Information on your child

Once your child is at school, you have the right to see virtually every record made about them. This includes details of your child's progress through the National Curriculum. There may also be information on your child's behaviour and reports by an educational psychologist. Parents have right of access to these records, although schools can withhold information which might refer to another pupil or which could cause harm to the pupil (for example, any reference to alleged or actual child abuse). Parents who wish to see their child's records should apply in writing to the governing body which must comply within fifteen days.

■ YOUR RIGHT TO CHOOSE

Your right to state your preference of school is set out in the Education Act 1980. You do not have to choose the nearest school and you are not required to give reasons for your choice at this stage. The law says local education authorities must meet parents' wishes unless there are specific reasons for not doing so. These might include the fact that a school is full to its physical limit or – in the case of selective schools – that the school is not educationally appropriate for your child.

You have the right to appeal if your child is not given a place at the school you have chosen. Your local education authority must explain the appeals procedure to you and you have the right to put your case. The hearing is private and informal. You may either argue your own case or you can ask someone else, such as a solicitor, to represent you.

The general advice is to give positive reasons why your child is best suited to the school you prefer rather than being negative about the school you have been allocated. If you win your case, the local education authority must comply. It cannot appeal. If you lose, you can appeal to the Ombudsman or to the Education Secretary. Around 15,000 appeals are heard each year and some 40 per cent go in favour of the parents.

PARENTS' RIGHTS WHEN CHOOSING SCHOOLS

The Education Act 1980
- gives parents the right to state their choice of school.
- says education authorities must comply unless there are specific reasons not to do so.
- gives parents the right to appeal.
- makes the appeal verdict binding on the education authority and school.
- gives parents the right to a further appeal to the Secretary of State.

The Education Reform Act 1988
- introduced 'open enrolment', preventing artificial limits on school numbers.
- set a 'standard number' of pupils for each school which reflects its physical capacity.
- requires schools to accept pupils up to that number.
- prevents education authorities discriminating against you just because you live across the border in another authority.

Each year, education authorities must publish details of their admissions arrangements. These must state how many pupils will be admitted and how places will be allocated if schools are oversubscribed. A typical education authority operates its admissions on the following criteria:

Admissions priorities
1 to children with a family association (i.e. brother or sister already at the school).
2 to children who might be affected by medical or family considerations (e.g. mobility difficulties).
3 to children for whom any alternative school would be further away.
4 to children whose home is nearer to the school.

Parents are free to apply to schools in education authorities other than the one they live in. In urban areas with several schools close together – such as London – this is common practice. Education authorities cannot discriminate against children from outside their areas. In December 1989, the Court of Appeal delivered what has become known as the 'Greenwich judgement' after a dispute involving Greenwich education authority. The Court ruled that where an

192

education authority prescribed distance from school as a criterion for distinguishing between applicants, it could not take into account the authority's own boundaries.

This ruling has caused widespread concern. It means that parents who pay local taxes to support popular schools may find they lose out to parents from neighbouring authorities who happen to live closer to the school in question. In 1991 there were two important test cases of the Greenwich judgement. Parents of children who lived just outside Bromley took the authority to court claiming they had been discriminated against after being denied places at schools in Bromley. The authority wanted to operate a 'local schools for local children' policy. In a mirror-image case, parents in Kingston-upon-Thames took their education authority to court for failing to discriminate in favour of local children in the allocation of places at the local selective grammar schools. In both cases the High Court decision upheld the Greenwich judgement.

So – unless there is a further change in the legal position – it is now clear that education authorities cannot discriminate against children from outside their area. In the case of grammar schools, where admission is on the basis of ability, this could lead to the position where more children attend from outside the local education authority than within it. For most schools, where distance is a key criterion, the main problem will be for those living at the margins of authorities. So parents considering moving house in order to get into a 'good' education authority, should think more about the distance from the school of their choice than whether or not they are inside the authority's boundaries.

■ HOW TO COMPLAIN

Unfortunately there will always be times when parents are unhappy with what is being provided by either their child's school or their local education authority. At school level, it is always best to discuss your concern with first your child's class teacher and then – if still unsatisfied – the head teacher. Do not be daunted: nearly all schools will welcome your interest in your child's education. Equally, it does not help to start off in an aggressive way as upset parents often do. You may have misunderstood the situation or you may find the school staff were unaware of the problem. Or it may be something which lies beyond their power or resources, in which case you may be able to gain their help in tackling the education authority.

If you are still not satisfied, remember you can also approach the school governors, who include representatives of parents. The school secretary will tell you how to contact them. Governors must also hold an annual meeting for parents and this is another opportunity for you to raise your concerns. If you still wish to take things further, then you can approach your local education authority. You can either do this directly or through your local councillors.

Exclusions

Perhaps the most difficult situation parents could ever have to deal with is when a school decides to suspend or even expel their child. This is now known as 'exclusion' and usually follows extremely bad behaviour or persistent breach of school rules. Pupils can be excluded from the school on a permanent basis or for a fixed period. The local education authority must find a replacement school. Parents have the right to appeal against an exclusion order.

If you appeal to the school's governors, they will set up an appeals panel of at least three governors. You have the right to make your case to them directly or to ask someone else (a solicitor, for example) to do so for you. The head teacher or other members of staff involved in the exclusion can give evidence to the panel but cannot sit on it. If you are not satisfied with the decision of the governing body, a further appeal to the local education authority is possible. Detailed guidance of the appeals procedure is available from your local education authority. However – in all aspects of exclusions – parents are probably well advised to think about the long-term difficulties for the child if they insist on the school taking them back. A new start may well be in the interests of both the pupil and the school.

■ RELIGION

Parents of children at maintained schools have the right to insist their child receives religious education in school and that they take part in an act of collective worship each day. The act of worship can be at any time during the school day and does not have to involve the whole school at once. In maintained schools both religious education and worship must be broadly Christian, while in voluntary-aided schools it will reflect the denominational nature of the school. However schools are allowed to apply for exemption from the requirement for worship to be broadly Christian if, for example, a large proportion of the pupils are from other religious groups. The law also allows individual acts of worship to be exempted from the requirement to be broadly Christian, providing that requirement is met taking the school term as a whole.

Parents still have the right to withdraw their children from religious education and collective worship. The school must be notified first. Under certain circumstances, they also have the right to arrange for them to be taught in accordance with their own religious views.

■ SPECIAL NEEDS

There are a substantial number of children who have special educational needs. Once expert committee estimated that about 20 per cent of pupils might have special needs at some time during their school life. These may arise from physical or mental disabilities or behavioural problems. The Education Act 1981 – based on the recommendations of the Warnock Committee – requires local education authorities to identify the special needs of children and to make appropriate provision for them. This can take place within mainstream schools, but in more severe cases this can also be in special schools, or special units attached to primary or secondary schools. In 1989 there were 1,800 special schools providing education for around 117,000 children.

If you think your child needs special help then the starting point is to discuss matters with your child's teacher or head teacher. Schools will have at least one teacher who has overall responsibility for special needs teaching. If the school is unable to meet your child's special needs, then either you or the school can approach the local education authority for a formal assessment of your child's needs. This is sometimes known as 'statementing', since it leads to a formal statement of the special help your child needs.

The assessment will be carried out by various experts, including educational psychologists. The statement from the education authority must show how it intends to meet the needs identified by the assessment. Parents are entitled to a copy of the statement and can appeal against it. It is not easy for parents to ensure that local education authorities are recommending the most appropriate provision. The authorities are in a difficult position, since they must provide any help which the statement says is necessary. So there is always the potential for an authority not to recommend help which it knows it cannot afford to provide.

There are many places parents can turn to for advice in this difficult and complicated area. The Advisory Centre for Education has a special telephone service on 071–354–8321 available from 2pm to 5pm from Monday to Friday. Other contacts include:

★ Children's Legal Centre, 20 Compton Terrace, London N1. Tel: 071–359–6251.

★ Independent Panel for Special Education Advice, 12 Marsh Road, Tillingham, Essex. Tel: 0621–779781.

★ Dyslexia Institute, 133 Gresham Road, Staines, Middlesex, TW18 2AJ. Tel: 0784–463935.

NATIONAL CURRICULUM BOOKLIST FOR 1992

■

LEVEL ONE

★ *Each Peach Pear Plum* Janet and Allan Ahlberg (Picture Puffin)
★ *Ten, Nine, Eight* Molly Bang (Julia MacRae Books, Picture Puffin)
★ *Mr Gumpy's Outing* John Burningham (Cape, Picture Puffin)
★ *Dear Zoo* Rod Campbell (Campbell Books, Picture Puffin)
★ *The Very Hungry Caterpillar* Eric Carle (Hamish Hamilton)
★ *Bet You Can't* Penny Dale (Walker Books)
★ *The Bears Who Went to the Seaside* Susanna Gretz (Blackie, Picture Puffin)
★ *Titch* Pat Hutchins (Bodley Head, Picture Puffin, Julia MacRae Books)
★ *The Baked Bean Queen* Rose Impey (Heinemann, Picture Puffin)
★ *Is Anyone Home?* Ron Maris (Julia MacRae Books, Picture Puffin)
★ *Not Now, Bernard* David McKee (Andersen Press, Sparrow Books)
★ *On Friday Something Funny Happened* John Prater (Picture Puffin)
★ *How Do I Put It On?* Shigeo Watanabe (Bodley Head, Picture Puffin)

LEVEL TWO

★ *Miss Dose the Doctor's Daughter* Allan Ahlberg (Puffin Books)
★ *Mr and Mrs Hay the Horse* Allan Ahlberg (Puffin Books, Viking)
★ *Peepo!* Janet and Allan Ahlberg (Picture Puffin, Viking)
★ *Mrs Wobble the Waitress* Allan Ahlberg (Puffin Books, Viking)
★ *The Bad-Tempered Ladybird* Eric Carle (Picture Puffin)
★ *But Martin!* June Counsel (Picture Corgi)
★ *New Clothes for Alex* Mary Dickinson (Deutsh, Hippo Books)
★ *Dogger* Shirley Hughes (Julia MacRae Books)
★ 'A List' from *Frog and Toad Together* Arnold Lobel (Puffin Books, Heimemann, Mammoth)
★ 'The Story' from *Frog and Toad are Friends* Arnold Lobel (Puffin Books, Heinemann, Mammoth)
★ 'Tomorrow' from *Days With Frog and Toad* Arnold Lobel (Puffin Books, Heinemann, Mammoth)

★ *Andrew's Bath* David McPhail (Blackie, Picture Puffin)
★ *All in One Piece* Jill Murphy (Walker Books)
★ *Whatever Next!* Jill Murphy (Picturemac, MacMillan Children's Books)

LEVEL THREE

★ *A Necklace of Raindrops* Joan Aiken (Cape, Puffin Books)
★ *No Jumping On the Bed* Tedd Arnold (Bodley Head, Pan Piper)
★ *Joe Giant's Missing Boot* Toni Goffe (Walker Books)
★ *Osa's Pride* Ann Grifalconi (Little, Brown)
★ *Greedy Zebra* Mwenye Hadithi (Hodder, Knight Books)
★ *The Lost Toys* Irina Hale (Picture Puffin)
★ *Katie Morag and the Two Grandmothers* Mairi Hedderwick (Bodley Head, Picture Lions, Oliver & Boyd)
★ *Old Bear* Jane Hissey (Hutchinson Children's Books, Red Fox)
★ *Joe's Cafe* Rose Impey (Orchard Books)
★ *The Mice Next Door* Anthony Knowles (MacMillan)
★ *Jam: A True Story* Margaret Mahy (Dent, Mammoth)
★ *What's The Time, Rory Wolf?* Gillian McClure (Deutsch)
★ *The Mice and the Clockwork Bus* Rodney Peppé (Viking, Picture Puffin)
★ *Shaker Lane* Alice Provensen (Julia MacRae Books, Walker Books)
★ *Tall Inside* Jean Richardson (Methuen Children's Books, Picture Puffin)
★*A Dog for Ben* Jean Richardson and Joanna Carey (Methuen Children's Books, Picture Puffin)
★ *The Bunk-Bed Bus* Frank Rodgers (Viking, Picture Puffin)
★ *A Pet for Mrs Arbuckle* Gwenda Smith and Ann James (Picture Puffin)
★ *Janine and the New Baby* Iolette Thomas (Deutsch, Mammoth)
★ *The Turtle and the Island* Barbara Ker Wilson (Frances Lincoln)

LEVEL FOUR

★ *The Moon's Revenge* Joan Aiken (Cape)
★ *A Bear Called Paddington* Michael Bond (Young Lions, Collins)
★ *Alice's Adventures in Wonderland* Lewis Carroll (Puffin Classics)
★ *Matilda* Roald Dahl (Cape, Puffin)
★ *The Dancing Tigers* Russell Hoban and David Gentleman (Cape, Red Fox)

★ *Seasons of Splendour – Tales, Myths and Legends of India* Madhur Jaffrey (Pavilion, Puffin)
★ *Stig of the Dump* Clive King (Viking)
★ *The Downhill Crocodile Whizz and Other Stories* Margaret Mahy (Dent, Puffin)
★ *Winnie the Pooh* A.A. Milne (Mammoth)
★ *West Indian Folk Tales* Philip Sherlock (Oxford University Press)
★ *Carbonel* Barbara Sleigh (Puffin)
★ *Charlotte's Web* E.B. White (Puffin, MacMillan)

NATIONAL CURRICULUM TIMETABLE

In each case subject regulations come into force in August

	KEY STAGE 1 (5–7)	KEY STAGE 2 (7–11)	KEY STAGE 3 (11–14)	KEY STAGE 4 (14–16)
ENGLISH	1989	1990	1990	1992
MATHEMATICS and SCIENCE	1989	1990	1989	1992
FOREIGN LANGUAGES	—	—	1992	1995
TECHNOLOGY	1990	1990	1990	1993
HISTORY and GEOGRAPHY	1991	1991	1991	1994
ART, MUSIC and PE	1992	1992	1992	1995

USEFUL ADDRESSES

■

NATIONAL BODIES

Department of Education and Science, Sanctuary Building, Great Smith Street, London, SW1P 3BT. Tel. 071–925–5000.

For HMI reports: Department of Education and Science, Publications Despatch Centre, Honeypot Lane, Stanmore, Middlesex HA7 1AZ. Tel: 081–952–2366.

National Curriculum Council, Albion Wharf, 25 Skeldergate, York YO1 2XL. Tel: 0904–622533.

School Examinations and Assessment Council, Information Section, Newcombe House, 45 Notting Hill Gate, London W11 3JB. Tel: 071–229–1234.

Business and Technology Education Council (BTEC), Central House, Upper Woburn Place, London WC1H 0HH. Tel: 071–388–3288.

City and Guilds of London Institute, 76 Portland Place, London W1N 4AA. Tel: 071–580–3050.

Royal Society of Arts (RSA), 8 John Adam Street, London WC2N 6AJ. Tel: 071–930–5115.

HELP FOR PARENTS

Advisory Centre for Education (charitable organisation giving advice to parents), 1B Aberdeen Studios, 22–24 Highbury Grove, London N5 2EA. Advice line (2–5 pm Monday to Friday). Tel: 071–354–8321.

City Technology Colleges Trust, 15 Young Street, London W8 5EH. Tel: 071–376–2511.

Education Otherwise (advice for parents thinking of educating children at home), 36 Kinross Road, Leamington Spa, Warwickshire CV32 7ES. Tel: 0926–886828.

Independent Panel for Special Education Advice (gives free advice on children with special needs), 12 March Road, Tillingham, Essex CM0 7SZ. Tel: 0621–779781.

Independent Schools Information Service (advice on fee-charging schools), 56 Buckingham Gate, London SW1E 6AG. Tel: 071–630–8793/4.

Reading and Language Information Centre, University of Reading, London Road, Reading RG1 5AQ. (Send stamped addressed envelope for reading list for various age groups.)

Children's Legal Centre, 20 Compton Terrace, London N1. Tel: 071–359–6251.

Dyslexia Institute, 133 Gresham Road, Staines, Middlesex TW18 2AJ. Tel: 0784–463935.

Common Entrance Board, Ashley Lane, Lymington, Hampshire SO41 9YR.

INDEX
■

sixteen-year-olds' tests
  summary 73–6
  art 178–9
  English 90–1
  foreign languages 123–4
  geography 156
  history 145
  mathematics 101–2
  music 171–2
  physical education 165
  science 115–16
  technology 133
sixth form colleges 8, 37, 180–1, 184
sixth forms 37, 49, 60, 180–1
Smith, David J. 41
sociology 59
Spanish 120, 121
speaking and listening skills 78–9,
  81–2, 83, 84, 86, 87, 88, 89, 90,
  91
  in foreign languages 123, 124
special educational needs 8, 2, 13, 23,
  24, 50, 189, 194–5
specialist teachers 53, 55
special schools 8, 24
spell-checkers, computer 84
spelling 36, 69, 75, 78, 80, 81, 84, 87,
  88, 89, 90, 91
sport 49, 157–65, 181
staff, responsibility for 13, 17
Standard Assessment Tasks (SATs)
  63, 67, 72, 87, 98, 99
Standing Advisory Committees on
  Religious Education 14
state schools *see* nursery; primary;
  secondary; special; voluntary
  schools
streaming by ability 29, 31, 93
subject-centred teaching 30–1, 54, 55,
  56
suspension of pupils 193
swimming 158–9, 160, 161

Taylor, Sir William 30–1
teacher assessments (of pupils) 61, 62,
  63, 87, 99

teacher governors 12
teachers 11, 30–1, 34, 58
teaching expertise, pooling of 53–4
teaching methods 29–36
technology 37, 42–6, 43, 45, 52, 53, 56,
  58, 92, 125–33
  summary of syllabus 125–7
  work and tests 127–33
  see also seven-; eleven-; fourteen-;
    sixteen-year-olds' tests
television 34, 35, 80, 81
Tertiary Colleges 9, 37, 180–1
tests 61–77 *see also under* individual
  subjects; seven-; eleven-;
  fourteen-; sixteen-year-olds' tests
timetables 43, 52, 56
Tomlinson, Sally 41
topic work 32, 54–5, 59, 82, 83,
  93
traditional teaching 29–32, 49, 59
Training and Enterprise Councils 182
transport and travel 12, 38, 188
truancy 189
TVEI (Technical and Vocational
  Education Initiative) 43

university 182, 183, 185
upper schools 8–9

verbal reasoning tests 9, 47
videos, and reading standards 34
vocational courses 184–6
voluntary help 33
voluntary schools 8, 16, 27

Warnock Committee 194
Welsh language 52, 66
Welsh Office, responsibilities 10–11
word processors 83, 84, 85
writing, teaching of 36, 56, 69, 78,
  80–1, 82–3, 84, 85, 86–7, 88, 89,
  90, 91 *see also* English
written tests 63, 64 *see also*
  SATs

Youth Training courses 45, 181, 182

Help your child with these other titles from BBC Books

Help Your Child with Maths edited by Angela Walsh
Help Your Child with Reading edited by Wendy Body
Help Your Child with Science Steve Pollock and Julian Marshall
The Blue Peter Green Book Lewis Bronze, Nick Heathcote and
    Peter Brown
Wildside on Rainforests Paul Appleby
Wildside on Rivers, Lakes and Wetlands Susan McMillan
Wildside on Oceans Nick Davies
Wildside on Woodlands Tess Lemmon
Play It Safe – The Complete Guide to Child Accident Prevention
    Dr Sara Levene